Eat
LIKE YOU
GIVE A DAMN
RECIPES FOR THE NEW
ETHICAL VEGAN

Michelle Schwegmann

Josh Hooten

BOOK PUBLISHING COMPANY // SUMMERTOWN, TENNESSEE

Library of Congress Cataloging-in-Publication Data

Schwegmann, Michelle.
Eat like you give a damn : recipes for the new ethical vegan / Michelle Schwegmann and Josh Hooten.
   pages cm
Includes index.
ISBN 978-1-57067-313-9 (pbk.) -- ISBN 978-1-57067-879-0 (e-book)
1. Veganism. 2. Vegan cooking. I. Hooten, Josh. II. Title.
TX392.S375 2015
641.5'636--dc23

2015010397

© 2015 Michelle Schwegmann
Food Photos © 2015 Josh Hooten & Michelle Schwegmann

Photographer: Josh Hooten
Food styling: Josh Hooten & Michelle Schwegmann
Cover and interior design: Josh Hooten
Author photo: Amy Gedgaudas

Pictured on front cover: Beet, Lettuce, Tempeh, and Avocado Sandwiches, p. 148; Only-Kale-Can-Save-Us-Now Salad, p. 83; Polenta Fries, p. 110.
Pictured on back cover: Chopped Salad with Spicy Hot Chickpeas, p. 84; Ruby's Tomato Soup, p. 96.

Book Publishing Company
PO Box 99
Summertown, TN 38483
888-260-8458
bookpubco.com

ISBN: 978-1-57067-313-9

Printed in the United States of America

20 19 18 17 16 15   1 2 3 4 5 6 7 8 9

Book Publishing Company is a member of Green Press Initiative. We chose to print this title on paper with 10% postconsumer recycled content, processed without chlorine, which saves the following natural resources:

10 trees
310 pounds of solid waste
4,622 gallons of water
852 pounds of greenhouse gases
4 million BTU's of energy

For more information on Green Press Initiative, visit greenpressinitiative.org.

Environmental impact estimates were made using the Environmental Defense Fund Paper Calculator. For more information visit papercalculator.org.

Printed on recycled paper.

Contents

Rescued piglets, Farm Sanctuary, Watkins Glen, NY.

The Reason

JUNE 29, 2011, was an unremarkable day in central Iowa. A low breeze clung to the earth, bending the tips of cornfields in unison. A cloudless sky pooled loosely around the sun, which dutifully illuminated what little the landscape offered it. Industrial fans, their hum so ubiquitous as to require more effort for the ear to grasp than it does to ignore, continued their charge pulling putrid air from inside thousands of metal sheds that warehoused the living, breathing, feeling bodies we identify as "food animals."

Before dawn, I packed the final contents of my hotel room, a dimly lit, single occupancy on the first floor of a Super 8 that had housed my undercover operation for nearly two months. I swung my Jetta south onto Highway 35 and let the dense Iowa air fill my lungs for a few wistful miles before making a hard left onto I-80, straight through to Illinois. By the time I arrived at the headquarters of Mercy for Animals (MFA), perched discreetly above a shoe store on Chicago's north side, the atmosphere in the office was electric. News was traveling quickly that an undercover investigator had gained employment at one of the largest factory pork farms in Iowa and documented cruelty, abuse, neglect, and incompetence so egregious that national grocery store chains had begun cutting ties with the company in light of the release.

The pork industry confines pigs in a way that bears no resemblance to their natural behavior.

Before dawn, I packed the final contents of my hotel room, a dimly lit, single occupancy on the first floor of a Super 8 that housed my undercover operation for nearly two months.

Pigs are curious, intelligent, active animals who live in matriarchal societies of several families. When they are intensively confined with no intellectual or social stimulation, forced to live in their own waste, divorced from their piglets, and subjected to a life in a cage that is barely bigger than their own bodies, they exhibit behavior typical of madness. I witnessed mother sows biting the bars of their cages in frustration and boredom, or rubbing their noses raw and bloody on the metal floor of their cages during attempts to "nest"—another natural instinct of pigs that farming doesn't allow for. Piglets in stress and boredom will chew the tails of their siblings, a behavior not found in any pig colonies outside the walls of factory farms. Tail biting is such a problem on pig farms that the industry has taken to tail docking, a procedure whereby they cut off the tails of infant piglets. This practice is accomplished with no more than sharp shears and a shot of iron to supplement the blood loss.

In addition to tail docking, Iowa Select was found to be castrating male piglets without anesthesia, commonly resulting in intestinal ruptures and slow death. Pregnant sows were confined in gestation crates—cages so small a grown pig cannot lie down, turn around, or escape her own waste for most of her adult life. Gestation crates are considered so cruel that they have been banned in the United Kingdom, New Zealand,

and Australia, and in several US states, including Florida and California. With the release of MFA's investigation, pork industry leaders came to the defense of Iowa Select, touting their practices as not only humane but also standard practice in the industry. Federal law contains a little-known legal loophole that protects farming activity that can be described as common industry practice. The pork industry was not only ready to defend Iowa Select, but by rallying around the institutional cruelty found there, they were also effectively ensuring the allowance of those practices at every other industrial hog farm in the country.

For their part, Iowa Select launched an "internal investigation" into the matter and, shockingly, found themselves in full compliance with their own standards of care. They quietly returned to business as usual, but not without first adding several lines to their employment applications asking candidates to disclose whether they were affiliated with any vegan or animal rights organizations and whether they intended to photograph any activity within Iowa Select without permission. The State of Iowa assisted in the effort by making it illegal to provide misleading answers on a job application, effectively eliminating employment-based undercover investigations in the state of Iowa—the largest pork- and egg-producing state in the country at the time of the release.

I had left my position at Iowa Select three days prior to the release, having obtained hundreds of hours of undercover footage detailing an institutional level of cruelty so deeply entrenched in the culture of industrial pork production that it has been found in equal measure at sow farms of all sizes across the United States and Canada, almost without exception. Investigators are routinely finding that industrial animal farms and slaughterhouses are incapable of self-regulation. As a backhanded testament to this reality, the industries themselves have taken grave new measures to curtail investigative activity on their farms. Instead of addressing the cruelty and neglect required to breed and slaughter animals at such an unsustainable level, factory farmers are targeting the whistleblowers who have brought farm abuse public. So-called Ag Gag laws have cropped up in several states, each hand-tailored to suppress whistleblowing activity and to ensure maximum protection for animal abusers by making it illegal to report what goes on inside their walls. Undercover investigations on factory farms have been so successful in turning consumers against the cruelty of animal production that the animal agriculture industry has made it clear it would rather target the first amendment rights of American citizens than entertain the notion of changing standard industry practice. Thanks to undercover investigations, more and more consumers are waking up to the realization that they cannot trust the word of the fox guarding the hen house.

At the time of my investigation, Iowa Select was the fourth largest pork producer in the United States and the largest in the state of Iowa. Far from being an isolated incident, the activity I found there every day was a well-documented snapshot of industrial pork production. These are common practices, defended by leaders in animal production, defended by our regulatory agencies, and horrifying enough to leave marks on my psyche so indelible that even three years later I wake from nightmares more often than I can admit aloud.

Where there are factory farms there is abuse, cruelty, and neglect. These are essential components to the success of animal factories and slaughterhouses. Without them it would be impossible to produce meat and animal by-products at the rate they are consumed. It is our duty to not only instigate change inside factory farms but to also simultaneously stem the tide of demand for their products by refusing to pay farmers to abuse animals on our behalf.

Before I became vegan, I saw the production of animals for food the way most people do—a brutish

Where there are factory farms there is abuse, cruelty, and neglect. These are essential components to the success of animal factories and slaughterhouses. Without them it would be impossible to produce meat and animal by-products at the rate they are consumed.

but necessary part of life on earth where humans have to eat, and what we eat are milk, eggs, and meat. I loved animals, such as the dogs I lived with, the horses I rode, and the deer I camped near in the woods of Washington State where I grew up, but I maintained a blurry separation between companion animals and food animals.

I scoffed at PETA leafleteers with righteous disdain and talked myself out of the creeping sadness I would feel when an undercover video from a factory farm would make the news. Without realizing it, I had allowed my compassion for animals to atrophy. My heart fractured into a world where there were animals I cared about and those I ate. This compartmentalization is no accident, and it is the mental device animal abusers are counting on us to use when we see their products at the grocery store.

Like a lot of people, I was easily swayed by the marketing campaigns that asserted that "humane" meat, milk, and eggs were better for animals than their industrial counterparts. The concept of "humane" animal products taps into the innate sense of compassion and aversion to cruelty we are all born with. I learned too late that "free range," "cage-free," and "humane" are purely marketing terms unregulated by any government agency and applied with impunity by companies looking to squeeze an extra dollar out of a carton of eggs by preying on the natural empathy we feel toward animals. It was that glimmer of understanding that opened the door for me to finally acknowledge that I didn't have to live in a world where cruelty was my only option.

Already deeply aware of institutionalized forms of human oppression, such as sexism, racism, classism, and homophobia, I considered myself a champion for the rights of others. I was unafraid to confront injustice wherever I saw it and alter my own behavior whenever necessary.

The random assignment of worth based on morally insignificant physical attributes is called speciesism—the oppression of others based on the characteristics of their species. We cannot choose our skin color; we cannot choose our chromosomes; and we cannot choose our species. We are not superior or inferior for having been born a human, a chicken, a piglet, or a turkey.

Through the work of philosophers such as Peter Singer and Carol Adams, I finally began to realize that just as we shouldn't accept race or gender as a basis for denial of equal treatment, we shouldn't accept species for the same purpose. The lightbulb went off. I realized that we discriminate against animals not because we are meant to eat them but because we decide to eat them, and we breed them exclusively for the pleasure of our palates. At that moment, finding myself in violation of an ethical truth as valid as any other I had been fighting for, I knew I could no longer participate in the imprisonment and slaughter of lives that were not mine to take.

It was a crushing, humiliating realization, one I felt deeply ashamed of for not arriving at sooner. It was also the discovery that I would have to change my lifestyle in ways that felt too huge, too incomprehensible in their scope to wrap my tired arms

Johnny, Farm Sanctuary, Orland, CA.

We are so lucky to live in a time when vegan alternatives to the meat-consuming status quo are so plentiful and are getting better by the day. I am constantly awed by the simple elegance of a ripe avocado or a life-affirming coconut-milk ice-cream sandwich.

around. I felt overwhelmed by the path forward and daunted by the knowledge that I could not go back, knowing what I now knew.

I didn't come to veganism with my head held high, ready to embrace my new awakening with clarity. I came to veganism embarrassed and ashamed of what I had participated in. I was a poor, broken soul, seeking refuge for a heart hardened by a world too painful, too cruel, and too vast in its complacency to bear alone. I felt the weight of hatred, oppression, injustice, and horrors too common in the depths of the human condition, and I felt them so acutely that emotional paralysis had claimed great swaths of my compassion and empathy. I didn't know where to begin, let alone how to move forward. I mean, what was I even going to eat now?

The powerful thing about choice is that it can both paralyze and liberate us. By finding a group of like-minded vegans who could hold my hand on those first trips to the grocery store, lend me their cookbooks, and introduce me to the animal welfare groups that would ultimately become my second family, I began to see veganism as a beacon of community—one that is founded on truth, compassion, beauty, and, yes, cupcakes. I slowly began to emotionally reconnect with animals. I allowed myself to cry when I encountered cruelty. I allowed myself to acknowledge that we are agents of action, and those actions have consequences for lives outside our own. I allowed myself to feel connected to those beings and recognize our shared experience in a way that compelled me to honor their sovereignty and acknowledge that they don't owe me their lives in exchange for their right to exist.

We often hear people outside the vegan community wonder what the earthly point is to farm animals if we don't eat them. The point of their lives, much like our own, is to live, and to feel, and to connect, and to be. Unadulterated by intervention. Unburdened by demand. Unmarred by oppression. I want for animals what I want for myself, because I can tell you that from the look in the eye of a mother sow as she struggles through a cage to comfort her tortured piglets, we are all animals, aching simply to be.

We are so lucky to live in a time when vegan alternatives to the meat-consuming status quo are so plentiful and are getting better by the day. I am constantly awed by the simple elegance of a ripe avocado or a life-affirming coconut-milk ice-cream sandwich. Some of the most beautiful dishes are those that honor the unassailable perfection of garlic, salt, lemon, and olive oil, while some of the most inspirational come from a weekend spent fussing over an attempt at home-cured cashew cheese.

Cooking is a culturally significant ritual, the richness of which cannot be understated. The way we cook for one another and ourselves is so deeply intertwined with our need for community, love, intimacy, hearth, and home. Food is what creates and nourishes us both physically and spiritually, and cooking is the language we use to communicate those values. The world we want is ours if we make it. **Let's get to work.**

ANONYMOUS
Former undercover investigator at Mercy for Animals

Foreword

It has never been easier to adopt a diet that honors compassion and a sense of purpose.

WHEN I FIRST MET Michelle and Josh, it was in their wonderful store Herbivore in Portland, Oregon. I was speaking on vegan nutrition at a conference and stopped by afterward to shop at the store I had heard so much about. I came away with some great vegan goodies—and with two new best friends. Surrounded by the fun and practical tools of a joyful vegan lifestyle, Josh and Michelle were warm and happy representatives of the way they eat and live. They truly give a damn.

It's been clear over the years that Michelle, Josh, and I bring very similar perspectives to our work: we want a world that is kinder to animals. We also want to make it as enjoyable, easy, and practical as possible for people to embrace that world, which includes having delicious plant-based food. And that's exactly what Michelle and Josh do through their store and through this book.

If you're just starting to eat in a way that makes a difference for animals, this is the cookbook that's going to make your transition smooth, uncomplicated, and fun. And if you've been vegan for a while but are always looking for new, easy meal ideas, you're going to love these recipes.

My own work focuses on pointing vegans toward food choices that ensure a balanced diet and optimal health. I'm a dietitian, so of course I'm all about nutrition. But we don't eat nutrients; we eat food. And this book is just what you need to find great menu ideas and recipes for fabulous meals that will help you stay healthy.

Not sure how to add legumes to your diet? Try the recipes for Apple & Peanut Butter Smoothie (page 15) or Diner Breakfast Tacos (page 30). If you're new to dark leafy greens, such as kale and collards, Michelle and Josh have super-easy tips on page 118 for preparing them. Experiment with nutritional yeast, rich in vitamin B12, by pouring Sage Gravy (page 23) over your next batch of mashed potatoes or sprinkling Yellow Rose Parmesan (page 50) over a platter of pasta. And when you need a treat, Michelle and Josh have you completely covered with healthy choices, such as Multigrain Apple Muffins (page 157); and for something a bit more decadent, try Fudgy Brownies (page 166).

It has never been easier to adopt a diet that honors compassion and a sense of purpose. Enjoy this delightful collection of recipes and enjoy your journey toward a new way of eating, one that embraces compassion, health, and just plain fun.

VIRGINIA MESSINA, MPH, RD

VEGAN NUTRITION IN A NUTSHELL
Following are some simple guidelines for healthy vegan eating:

Eat legumes. This food group includes a variety of foods—not just beans, but also peanuts and peanut butter and all types of soy foods, such as tofu, tempeh, and soy milk. All of these foods are protein powerhouses. If you've ever worried about whether you'll get enough protein on a vegan diet, legumes are a big part of the answer. Include at least three servings per day and you'll never have to worry about meeting protein needs.

Pile your plate with a mountain of fruits and vegetables. You already know that these foods are good for you. They are nutrient dense (that is, they have lots of nutrition with minimal calories) and they are packed with phytochemicals that can protect against chronic disease. There are a few extra advantages too. When we choose fruits and veggies that are high in vitamin C, the iron in our meals is more readily absorbed. Deep-orange vegetables (such as carrots and winter squash) and dark leafy greens are great sources of vitamin A.

Choose healthy fats. Fat has developed a pretty bad reputation over the years and it's completely undeserved. The truth is that some fats are unhealthy (mostly the ones found in animal foods), but some are good for you. Higher-fat foods, such as nuts, for example, protect the health of your heart. Seeds can be a good source of essential minerals, such as zinc. Diets that include olive oil are linked to lower risk for disease. And some higher-fat foods—walnuts, flaxseeds, canola oil, and hemp seed oil—are important sources of essential omega-3 fats.

The key is not to go crazy with these higher-calorie foods. Snacking all day on nuts can drive your calorie intake up too high, but a sprinkle of nuts on a salad or stirred into cooked grains is always a good choice. And a teaspoon or so of a healthy oil in a salad dressing or to sauté veggies can enhance the flavors of food.

Get plenty of calcium. Did you grow up like I did, guzzling milk for healthy bones? My mom didn't know any other way to ensure enough calcium in my diet. And frankly, I didn't either, even in my early days as a dietitian. Now we recognize that many healthy foods are naturally rich in calcium. Certain leafy greens, such as collards and kale, are excellent sources of calcium. You can even get calcium from navel oranges and figs. We also have access to many calcium-fortified foods, including plant milks made from soybeans, almonds, cashews, and hemp seeds.

Choose foods fortified with vitamin D. Most people, vegan or not, would be hard pressed to get enough vitamin D from their food. Very few foods are natural sources of vitamin D, which is why items such as cow's milk and breakfast cereals are fortified with it. Technically, vitamin D shouldn't be such a big deal since we can make it when our skin is exposed to sunlight. But many people don't make enough. For example, older people need a lot more sunlight and so do people with darker skin. Smog, clouds, and sunscreen all interfere with vitamin D synthesis, so supplements or fortified foods, such as plant milks, can be good insurance.

Pop a pill for vitamin B12. Because vitamin B12 is found only in animal foods, it's essential that vegans take a supplement or use fortified foods. I take a daily supplement providing 100 micrograms of B12 because that's just easiest for me. But you can use fortified foods or cook with nutritional yeast to get enough B12 in your diet too.

Enjoy some treats. When you eat in a way that honors animals, you end up with a few personal benefits as well. Vegans typically have lower blood pressure and lower blood cholesterol levels, and we are less likely to develop type 2 diabetes. Whole plant foods are good for you, there is no doubt about that. But what would life be without dessert?

Fortunately, you can eat in a way that protects animals, the planet, and the health of your body and still have a few treats. So if you like brownies and apple pie—and who doesn't?—don't think that going vegan means you need to give up those things. Build most of your diet around whole plant foods and enjoy some treats now and then.

The Birth of Herbivore

HERBIVORE BEGAN IN 2002, in our spare bedroom, because Josh needed new T-shirts. He had been looking for a stylish animal-rights T-shirt for some time. He couldn't find anything that satisfied his snobby visual aesthetic and not-really-in-your-face-but-still-committed nature. Being a graphic designer, as well as being raised on the legendary punk band Fugazi and the DIY ethic of the nineties punk rock scene, the solution to the problem was obvious: make our own.

We came up with our company name, Herbivore, although Michelle was convinced it would lead people to think we were hippies selling weed. We made our first design, "Vegetarianism is for Lovers" (the word "vegan," we thought, would be kind of extreme back then—ha!). Then we built a website and, since this was pre-Myspace (look it up, young people) and pre-Facebook, we spread the message as best we could. We sold a few shirts, which covered our initial outlay. It was just enough for us to feel encouraged.

Josh learned screen printing to help keep our costs down, and we created a second design, "Praise Seitan." We sold a few of those too . . . and also received a few angry letters. We realized that there were other people who shared our sense of humor, design aesthetic, and ethics. We were elated!

We opened a business bank account, created more designs, and very slowly grew Herbivore. In 2006, we felt that we were on steady enough ground for Michelle to finally quit her job, and we turned the front of our office space into a tiny retail store. We've both been working at Herbivore full time ever since. In November 2007, after a year in our tiny location, we moved and helped open Portland's vegan mini-mall along with our friends Sweetpea Baking Company, Food Fight! Vegan Grocery, and Scapegoat Tattoo.

One of the best parts of running this company is the freedom it gives us to take on new projects and follow our interests. Over the years, we've been involved with numerous related activities, including organizing animal rights conferences, publishing books and a magazine, and hosting a wide variety of events at the store. The book you're holding is the result of this freedom and our desire to find new ways to help animals.

While it's great to be able to take on any kind of creative project we're interested in, since our very first design we made it a priority to spread the word about animal rights. We use the respected voice of our business to speak up for animals, we donate design work and products to major and many small-scale animal rights and social justice groups, and we do direct fund-raising year after year. The number of groups, people, and campaigns we've supported is in the hundreds. Even more than that, we're proud that as of this writing, we've helped to raise over $125,000 for animal sanctuaries. Although it's very gratifying to make a living from our hard work, it's equally important that we give back to the movement that supports us. We exist to put an end to animal suffering, but we aren't done yet.

Why I'm Vegan

MICHELLE

When Josh and I met, he had just become vegan, and I was an omnivore who had briefly dabbled in vegetarianism during high school. I had been a cheese, French fry, and bagel vegetarian; hence, the brevity. I wanted Josh to be vegetarian, not vegan, so it would be easier for us to eat out. I pestered him about that all the time, but he never pestered me about my animal-eating ways. This went on for almost a year. Eventually, we struck a deal: he would go back to being just vegetarian if I read *Diet for a New America* by John Robbins (which was the book that had inspired Josh to become vegan.) He said that if I read that book and still wanted him to no longer be vegan, he would only have vegan meals occasionally to make things easier for me. Well, I read the book, was outraged when I learned the truth about the foods I had eaten all my life, and immediately became vegetarian. Josh, of course, remained vegan. He had tricked me!

But I still resisted veganism. I was addicted to cheese, and to be completely honest, I also considered veganism too "extreme" for me. It was difficult to accept that what I had considered to be true my whole life—that eating meat, dairy products, and eggs is healthy and acceptable— was nothing more than a carefully fabricated but well-promoted lie. Instead, I rationalized my actions, even though I knew better. I became really good at deceiving myself. I wanted what tasted good, what was familiar and convenient, and what pleased me. Besides, how could it be so wrong to eat these things if everyone

else was too? Then, about two years later, I finally woke up and realized how much effort it was taking to lie to myself and how silly it was to buy animal products when vegan versions were so readily available. So I stopped doing both—cold. I came home from work one day and simply told Josh, "I'm vegan now!"

It feels great that my actions align 100 percent with my beliefs. Once I decided to change my behavior, it was easy to see that all I had to do was change my habits. And with so many amazing vegan foods popping up these days, I don't miss cheese or any other animal products one bit.

JOSH

I became vegan in 1999, after a short stint as a reluctant vegetarian. I followed a vegetarian diet when I lived in Boston, partly because my dog at the time made me think harder than I ever had before about why I was eating animals. Why was it okay for me to eat one animal but not another? Why did the idea of eating my dog repulse me but the idea of eating, say, a pig, who is equally as gentle, intelligent, and sociable not bother me at all?

All my friends were vegetarian, but they didn't pressure me in any way. I was just embarrassed to eat meat in front of them because I knew they were doing something good and I wasn't because I was lazy. I knew they were smarter than I was and that what they were doing had merit. So, eventually I joined them.

Then I moved to Chicago, and while most of my new friends were vegetarian, not one was vegan. I started to think about my own health more and about what I ate. I realized I was happy that I didn't eat animals, but I wasn't fully aware of the ethical issues involved. Up until then, vegetarianism had always been mostly a social choice for me. I decided to learn more about meat production, so I read the John Robbins classic, *Diet for a New America*. I remember finishing the chapter about egg production and realizing how cruel it was. I knew I had to become vegan right then. I wasn't particularly excited about this. I felt that the effort would be monumental—that I would become a social pariah and never be able to eat out again. I thought I'd spend the best years of my life reading labels on food packages at the grocery store and cooking everything from scratch (even though I didn't know how to cook). As daunting as it felt, I knew I had no choice. The curtain had been pulled back, and I saw the truth about the food I ate. I couldn't unsee that, and I've been vegan ever since.

It took a few weeks to get used to the change, and a few months to start feeling confident saying I was vegan, but once I'd made the transition, I was happy I'd done it. There was no reason to ever look back.

Veganism is the New Normal

WELCOME! IF YOU'VE HAD it with animal products but are unsure what to eat now, you've picked up the right book. If you love Herbivore Clothing and our designs, we hope you'll love the food we make too. Whoever you are, with this book you'll get a glimpse into my life and kitchen and the lives of Josh and our daughter, Ruby; collectively, we've been vegan for 252 dog years. We love being vegan. We love helping people transition to veganism. And we love eating. We are honored to share our favorite recipes with you, along with some basic tips and tricks to help you succeed in becoming a full-fledged Herbivore. But first, let's talk a little bit about what "normal" is.

In the Western world, it's considered "normal" to eat the body parts of various animals throughout the day. It's "normal" for people to eat just one kind of vegetable a day: deep-fried potatoes. It's "normal" for people to dote on their cats or dogs while eating parts of a pig. It's "normal" to eat a hamburger containing meat that could have come from as many as a hundred different cows. It's "normal" to follow the status quo and not question what's on your plate, and it's socially unacceptable to decline animal products.

Let me say it loud and proud: choosing to not eat animals is the most logical, sensible, and yes, normal choice you can make. You simply have to update your definition of "normal" and then develop a new set of habits and stick with them. What now may seem confusing or even a bit scary will eventually become your new normal. Soon you'll be veganizing recipes and sharing them with friends. Ask for help if you need it, use the resources we recommend (see page 174), and don't give up if you don't love vegan cheese the first time you try it.

Let's be honest: vegan alternatives aren't going to taste exactly like their animal-based predecessors. But if you give them half a chance, you'll find that the cruelty-free versions will scratch the same itch, and before you know it, you will prefer them. And as a bonus, they're a healthy and compassionate choice too.

Okay, time to end the serious stuff. Let's talk about cooking!

I love to cook. Making food is relaxing, fun, and rewarding for me. However, I'm fully aware that some people hate to cook and, well, that sucks. But since you picked up this book, I trust that you don't think cooking is torture. Which means that it might not be such a stretch to tell you that when you eat more vegetables, you have to chop more vegetables, and that takes a little bit of time and effort. But the results are so worth it! Food preparation can be private and meditative, or it can be done with friends and family, and you can share the delicious rewards when you're finished.

For the past several years, I've been cooking with cast iron pans. Cast iron is enjoying a revival, and with good reason. Cast iron cookware is inexpensive, durable as hell, and if seasoned and treated properly, develops a naturally nonstick interior. Do a little research about how to care for cast iron, invest in a skillet or two, and give it a try. There's no need to buy costly pots and pans to get rolling with vegan cooking. Sure, fancy cookware comes in beautiful colors and looks pretty in blog posts, but a grocery-store pan is going to be just as fabulous.

Because I want your dishes to be amazing the first time (and every time) you make them, please read each recipe in its entirety before you begin. It will be well worth your time. If you're new to cooking, make a recipe as written the first time, and then customize it to your tastes the next time. If you're experienced in the kitchen, go wild! Think of these recipes as a jumping-off point. We want you to create food that you'll love to eat, and you know best what rings your bell. Adapt! Be inspired! Eat like you give a damn!

Give a Damn...

EAT LIKE YOU GIVE A DAMN ABOUT YOUR HEALTH

Neither Josh nor I have a degree in nutrition, and we're in no way experts on specific nutritional requirements. We also don't promote veganism as a panacea for health challenges. We believe veganism is an ethical choice that may have health benefits (emphasis on "may"). That's because who knows what you're buying at the store and eating at two in the morning when you get the munchies! It's possible to be as unhealthy on a vegan diet as it is on a diet packed with meat, cheese, and eggs.

Here is what we do know: The Academy of Nutrition and Dietetics states that appropriately planned vegan diets are fine for all people, at all stages of life. That sounds pretty definitive to us Herbivores! But, of course, there's a catch: "appropriately planned." What does that mean? Do meat eaters have appropriately planned diets? Looking around, that obviously isn't the case. The sheer number of diet books and fad diets coming out every year tells us that most people have no idea what to eat. Information is contradictory, experts argue, and opinions differ, even among vegan health professionals.

When you go vegan for ethical reasons, you're not going on a diet. Instead, you're taking a stand. But you still gotta eat, and you should go about it in a healthy way. It's your job to educate yourself and to eat an ethical diet you can feel good about.

There are many resources (see page 174) we recommend that you can turn to. Find a source you trust, and don't be shy about asking questions.

Our recipes are created to be vegan, delicious, varied, and satisfying for everyone. Many are quite healthful—some more than others. But, hey, we don't eat cookies and mac and cheese every day. We also don't think that everyone needs to fast or cleanse or eat all raw foods, drink green juice, be gluten-free or avoid soy (unless you have an allergy, of course), and never eat any oil or processed foods. Those are diets. If you want to be on one of those diets, there are books available for you. This is not a book pushing a diet; this is a book pushing an ethic. This is a book meant to support your choice to not eat animal products for ethical reasons by giving you recipes for vegan food so good that you'll take one bite, look at your friends, and say, "Oh my gawd! This is freakin' awesome!"

EAT LIKE YOU GIVE A DAMN ABOUT THE PLANET

You probably have heard about the devastating effects animal agriculture has on the environment. Perhaps you've heard the phrase "real environmentalists don't eat meat." Both statements are no joke.

Animal agriculture is the leading cause of global warming, according to "Livestock's Long Shadow," a 2006 report by the Food and Agricultural Organization of the United Nations. The combined assaults on the earth include the animals' production of methane gas, feedlot runoff that contaminates waterways, soil erosion, inefficient use of water and food for farmed animals, transport fuel, and more. The single largest cause of deforestation in the Amazon is the conversion of the land to pasture for livestock or to grow crops to be fed to livestock.

Should we be grateful that there's grass-fed beef? Nope. Grass-fed cattle produce one-third more methane than grain-fed cattle and require much more land and water. Don't be fooled by slick marketing.

There are many, many ways all of us can lessen our impact on this planet. Not eating animals is by far the most effective thing you can do to for the environment.

EAT LIKE YOU GIVE A DAMN ABOUT YOUR FELLOW HUMANS

In an article published in the *Washington Post* in 2005 called "Meatpacking's Human Toll," Jamie Fellner, the US program director for Human Rights Watch, and Lance Compa, author of a Human Rights Watch report on meat and poultry workers, stated the following: "Working conditions in US meat and poultry plants should trouble the conscience of every American who eats beef, pork, or chicken."

Meatpacking plants are the most dangerous factory jobs in the United States, with rates of injury (which include repetitive motion injuries, cuts, dismemberment, and limbs being crushed in machinery) three times higher than any other industry. The largely immigrant workforce in slaughterhouses have almost no rights, and mistreatment and exploitation are common. These low-paying, high-risk jobs put corporate profits above human rights so egregiously that Human Rights Watch (which usually spends its time monitoring abuses in war zones, and that should tell you something) stated the jobs violated international agreements promising a safe workplace. The Food Empowerment Project has documented workers describing unsanitary and unsafe work environments as well as an atmosphere of intimidation and fear about reporting those conditions and risk being demoted or terminated.

ABOUT YOURSELF

When I went vegan, I was completely overwhelmed at first. What do I do with my leather shoes? What are all these ingredients in this bread? What am I going to say when people want to argue with me about eating animals? How am I going to eat out with non-vegan friends? It was a lot to think about, and I definitely felt as though I'd just put a huge weight on myself. I was committed to my decision, so I knew I'd figure it out, but I feared I was in over my head. Perhaps you feel this way too.

Luckily, we promise you will get over the initial feeling of being overwhelmed. Media today makes it simple to find like-minded friends! Find blogs you identify with. Join or start a local group. And if you live in an isolated place or don't have a support network, online groups are the perfect answer. We have so many friends from the Internet! There has never been an easier time to live a cruelty-free lifestyle. May the links you click lead you to finding your own favorite vegan blogs and voices!

The first couple of weeks being vegan can be confusing but also exciting. We see a lot of new vegans at our store, and we always tell people it's not about perfection. It's okay to bumble through explanations of why you are vegan or accidentally eat food with "hidden" animal ingredients. You know what? It happens to all vegans, even us, fifteen years later. It's not about perfection; just do your best based on the information you have. The more you learn, the better you'll get at knowing what is and isn't vegan, and the easier it will become. You will find your own voice!

You'll quickly learn which products to buy and which restaurants in your area have vegan options and which don't. Soon you'll be an expert. It's true! And if you have people in your life who challenge your decision and you aren't good at reciting a bunch of facts and figures under pressure, just say that you're following your heart, and your heart tells you that eating animals is wrong, so you aren't doing it anymore. Keep building that support network; social support is the most useful tool there is to staying vegan. And above all, be kind to yourself. You are doing something amazing for the animals, yourself, the planet, and your fellow human beings. Not getting it exactly right at first still means you're getting it mostly right, and that's huge.

The Vegan Debater's FAQ

HERE IS YOUR QUICKIE response sheet to the inevitable questions and comments most vegans hear at some point.

Q: Don't you care about plants? Plants have feelings too.
A: Plants don't have a central nervous system or a brain to process outside stimuli into what we would call "feelings." Even if it were true that plants have feelings, far fewer plants are needed when eaten directly by people than they are when they're fed to animals.

Q: Humans evolved to eat meat. That's why we have canine teeth.
A: If humans were natural carnivores, we would salivate at the smell of blood and the site of a dead animal. Give those teeth another good look. Do you really think they could rip through the hide of a wooly mammoth?

Q: Where do you get your protein?
A: I get my protein from the same place that big, strong animals, such as cows and elephants, do—from plants.

Q: Milk is important for strong bones. How can you get enough calcium without it?
A: Calcium is abundantly available in plant foods, including beans and dark leafy greens. Plants are also where large herbivores, such as elephants and, yes, even cattle, get their calcium.

Q: God put animals here for us to eat.
A: Why would any deity create living beings just so they could suffer horribly, as they do in our food industries? It seems more likely a deity would want people to eat the plants he or she created, because plants don't suffer.

Q: I've always eaten meat, so how can it be wrong?
A: Just because something is a tradition or has existed for a long time doesn't make it right. Humans have a long history of war, rape, and murder, but most of us believe these things are wrong.

Q: But meat tastes so good.
A: Agreed. That's why we eat vegan bacon every chance we get. You can replace almost any animal-based food with a vegan version, and you'll get all the flavor without the suffering, death, and environmental destruction.

Q: It's okay for me to eat a little meat. A little doesn't matter.
A: It most certainly matters to the animal you're eating. Believing that "a little" doesn't hurt is the same as saying that a little murder or child abuse is okay too.

Q: Why are vegans so preachy?
A: The compassion vegans feel for other animals might lead some of us to be less-than-ideal ambassadors for the movement. But that really isn't as common as many opposers make it out to be. In addition, there is always something to learn from a passionate person telling you how they feel.

Q: Animals eat other animals, so it's natural for us to eat animals too.
A: If it's so natural to eat other animals, we would instinctively hunt and kill them with our bare hands and tear their bodies apart with our teeth, not buy their body parts in plastic-wrapped Styrofoam packages and use euphemisms, such as "pork" and "beef," to refer to them.

Q: I could never give up cheese!
A: We understand, and it's probably because you're addicted to it. Just Google the word "casomorphin" and you'll understand why. You can break that addiction the same way you can any other addiction—just stop having it.

Q: What would happen to all the cows and pigs if we didn't eat them?
A: Eventually they would no longer exist because humans wouldn't be artificially inseminating millions of animals to create billions more animals just so we can eat them. We'd be in a far more natural state if we weren't breeding all these animals to eat, wear, and test on.

Q: It's fine for you, but I could never do it.
A: Of course you could. Veganism is simply the belief that humans aren't superior to other animals, just as men aren't superior to women, straight people aren't superior to gay people, and white people aren't superior to people of color. If you believe that all people should be free of oppression and suffering, it's not hard to expand that circle of compassion to include other animals.

Raising Vegan Kids

FIRST, LET'S GET THE HEALTH issue out of the way: the Academy of Nutrition and Dietetics and the American Academy of Pediatrics both state that vegan diets can provide all the nutrients pregnant vegans and vegan children need. It's vital to take the nutrition of your children (and yourself) very seriously. Therefore, rest assured that well-planned vegan diets can meet both your and your children's needs. It's confusing and sad how so many people assume that the standard American diet, laden with meat and animal products, provides babies and mothers with adequate nutrition, but that a diet based on fruits, vegetables, beans, and grains is considered insufficient, dangerous, and outlandish. Fortunately, there are excellent sources that cover vegan nutritional requirements for pregnant women, babies, and children (see Resources, page 174).

Second, the more popular that veganism becomes, the more that critics come out of the woodwork to share their lack of knowledge with you. Most of the time, folks haven't thought through what they're saying before they say it (and believe us when we tell you that we've heard it all!). Our favorite comment is this classic: "You shouldn't push your beliefs on your kids." Parents make all the decisions for young children, and naturally our decisions are going to reflect our values. This is true of every other parent, vegan or not. We're all for letting our daughter make decisions for herself when appropriate, but until she's old enough to do that in all areas of her life, we get to decide. We've taught our daughter, Ruby, to be vegan because we think it's the best path in life, just as

we're teaching her other important things, such as how to read, write, and swim.

We've also heard people express concern about raising a kid who's different from everybody else. If we lived in a place where everybody was racist or homophobic, we wouldn't teach our daughter to be racist or homophobic just so she would fit in. Parents teach what they believe is

right and wrong, so we are teaching our daughter how to stand up for her beliefs and defend her innate compassion for animals. Being different in that context is totally positive, even if it might be difficult to challenge the status quo.

So often we talk with other vegan parents and pregnant vegans about what and how much to tell children about veganism and animal issues. We have always been very honest with Ruby about why we are vegan. At first we were apprehensive to tell her how animals are killed and how their body parts are eaten and used, but she wanted to know. She was curious. She was sad. She had and still has lots of questions, but she completely understands. Of course, we keep everything age appropriate and find that simple and direct answers, without a lot of detail, are usually enough. If she wants to know more, she can ask.

We have also made it a point to make sure Ruby gets to meet and know animals that are typically raised for food. We are lucky enough to live near a number of animal sanctuaries that we can visit several times a year. Ruby has been around cows, chickens, pigs, goats, geese, and other farm animals her whole life. This is invaluable because it takes animals off the screen or page and makes them living, breathing creatures with whom she can interact. Meeting animals in person takes veganism from an abstract concept to reality. She can see that these animals have a personality, just like her dogs.

We believe that many people underestimate the capacity children have to understand and work with difficult information. And while much of the information about animal suffering is heartbreaking, it's never been something that Ruby can't handle, and knowing the truth very early in life will benefit her forever.

Above all, remember that you are raising a human who is naturally compassionate, and you want that human to be prepared to live in the world with awareness, kindness, and conviction.

It's Okay for Vegans to Love Meat and Cheese

SAY WHAT? There's a misconception that vegans eat like rabbits, munching on giant carrots and eating plain lettuce. While many of us love salad and make unusual treats with them, such as carrot bacon and carrot fries (Google them; they're for real, and real good!), the fact is that the great majority of vegans loved eating meat at one time and loved eating cheese before they became vegan. They just couldn't stomach the cruelty that went along with these foods, and that's why they gave them up.

But changing our diets doesn't stop our taste buds from still craving the foods we enjoyed prior to becoming vegan. That's why vegan burgers, meatballs, bacon, chicken, fish, ham, tuna, and similar kinds of products were developed. It's also why vegans have worked tirelessly to create vegan cheeses that melt and are rich, creamy, and delicious. Vegans are clearly a very inventive bunch!

But what is it about meat and cheese that we love so much? For some people, it's about keeping a tradition and igniting fond childhood memories. For others, it's a desire to eat familiar foods, fit in, and be like everyone else. For still others, it's more about the texture, smell, and rich flavors, which more often than not have to do with the fat and salt content of a dish. Thick slices of barbecue with a messy sauce can be great, but vegans want it to be made from seitan, not a cow. It still smells and tastes like barbecue!

But really, what does "meat" mean anyway? A mushroom is meaty. Peaches, tomatoes, avocados, mangoes, and coconuts have flesh. The inside of a nut is called the meat. Seitan is known as wheat meat. Expanding the concept of meat away from animals to include plant foods of all kinds opens the door to a world of different, exciting, and uncompromising meaty options.

The Herbivore's Cupboard

THERE ARE SOME INGREDIENTS used in the recipes in this book that you may not be familiar with. They are available at natural food stores and well-stocked supermarkets, and of course you can buy anything online. Read on to become an expert in these essential vegan ingredients.

AGAVE NECTAR: Agave nectar is a liquid sweetener that many vegans substitute for honey. Although agave nectar and honey have a similar consistency, agave nectar is slightly sweeter, so you can use less of it than you would honey.

ALMOND MEAL: Also known as almond flour, almond meal is made from almonds that are very finely ground until they have the texture of flour.

BROWN RICE FLOUR: Made from ground brown rice, brown rice flour is gluten-free and has a hearty, nutty flavor.

BROWN RICE SYRUP: Brown rice syrup is a thick, sticky, mild sweetener made by culturing cooked brown rice. It's about half as sweet as sugar.

CHICKPEA FLOUR: Also known as besan, gram flour, and garbanzo bean flour, chickpea flour is made from ground chickpeas.

COCONUT FLAKES: Coconut flakes are made from dried coconut meat. The recipes in this book call for unsweetened large coconut flakes.

FARRO: Farro is a hearty, heirloom grain that has been credited with being the original ancestor to modern-day wheat. It has a firm, chewy texture and nutty flavor.

FLAX MEAL: Flax meal is made from ground flaxseeds. It's typically used as an egg replacer, binder, and thickener, especially in baked goods.

HEMP SEEDS: Hemp seeds are the edible part of the hemp plant. They are smaller than sesame seeds and round (rather than elliptical). In addition to their pleasant crunch and nutty flavor, they are rich in healthy omega-3 fats.

MISO: Miso is a thick, salty, fermented paste made from soybeans or other legumes and rice or other grains. It adds umami to vegan dishes. Look for miso in the refrigerated section of natural food stores. It comes in many varieties (from light to dark); we prefer the lighter, more mellow kinds.

NUT OR SEED BUTTER: Nut and seed butters are pastes made from finely ground nuts or seeds. Peanut butter is the most renowned (although peanuts are technically legumes, not nuts), but there are many others. Try butters made from almonds, cashew nuts, hazelnuts, sesame seeds (sesame butter is known as tahini), sunflower seeds, pumpkin seeds, or hemp seeds.

NUTRITIONAL YEAST FLAKES: Fondly known as "nooch," nutritional yeast is made from toasted, deactivated yeast. The nutty, cheesy flavor of nutritional yeast has made it a favorite recipe ingredient and condiment. It's high in protein and B vitamins and is a staple in every Herbivore's kitchen. Nutritional yeast is available either powdered or flaked; we prefer the flakes and use them exclusively in our recipes. Store nutritional yeast in a sealed container at room temperature. It will keep indefinitely.

SEITAN: Believe me, we know seitan can be confusing! Let's demystify some things about it, shall we? First, it's pronounced say-TAN (not Satan, as in the devil). It's made from gluten, the protein in wheat that remains after the starch has been rinsed away. Seitan is a hearty, chewy food that resembles meat in taste and texture and can be used in recipes in much the same way. Although it's sometimes called wheat meat, we prefer the term "grain meat" because seitan is made from grain (that is, wheat). Also see "vital wheat gluten" below.

SMOKED PAPRIKA: A Spanish paprika that has a sweet and smoky flavor, smoked paprika is available at specialty spice shops and gourmet stores and from online retailers.

SOY CURLS: Made from defatted, non-GMO soybeans, Soy Curls are manufactured by Butler Foods. They are high in protein and fiber and are gluten-free. Soy Curls come dehydrated and can quickly be reconstituted in water or vegetable broth. The texture is incredibly meaty.

TAHINI: Tahini, also called tahini paste, is a butter made from finely ground sesame seeds. We prefer roasted tahini (made with roasted sesame seeds) rather than raw tahini (made with unroasted seeds), as it's much more flavorful. Look for Arabic brands, since they have a much better taste. When tahini is blended with other ingredients, it creates a luscious sauce (see Tahini Sauce, page 45).

TAMARI, REDUCED-SODIUM: Tamari is a liquid made from fermented soybeans. It's similar to soy sauce except it contains no wheat

and is typically more flavorful. Look for organic, reduced-sodium tamari, which contains all the flavor but has much less sodium.

VEGAN BUTTER: Vegan butter is a buttery tasting spread made from of a variety of plant oils. A common, popular brand is Earth Balance Vegan Buttery Spread.

VITAL WHEAT GLUTEN: Vital wheat gluten is the concentrated protein in wheat. During processing, the starch is removed from wheat flour and the gluten that is left behind is dried and powdered, resulting in a product that looks similar to flour. Vital wheat gluten is used in many commercially prepared vegan meat products and is the primary ingredient used in seitan. It is not the same as high-gluten flour (which is used to make bread rise higher).

WHITE WHOLE WHEAT FLOUR: Made from a special strain of wheat, white whole wheat flour has a mild flavor and lighter color and taste than standard whole wheat flour. It makes more attractive, less dense baked goods than its conventional counterpart.

ZA'ATAR: A Middle Eastern spice blend that typically contains basil, oregano, thyme, sumac, and sesame seeds is called za'atar. Mixtures of za'atar will vary according to the specific regions in which they were made.

How to Tofu (and Tempeh)

I WANT TO MAKE YOU love tofu (and tempeh) as much as I do. So if you're going to love it, you need to understand it. The follow contains all the pertinent information you need to make tofu so delicious you can't wait to sink your teeth into it.

TYPES OF TOFU

Although there are various kinds of tofu, the primary difference among them is the water content. Silken tofu has a high water content and is very creamy; it's mainly used for sauces, dips, and dressings. The firmest regular (not silken) tofu has very little water and can be easily sliced. It's great for marinating and creating chewy, meaty slices that can be grilled.

SILKEN TOFU

Silken tofu is available soft, firm, and extra-firm, but they are all primarily used for sauces, puddings, dressings, and other creamy foods. Mori-Nu brand silken tofu comes in aseptic packages that can be conveniently stored in the pantry for several months. Other brands come in hard plastic containers that are sealed with plastic film. These types must be stored in the refrigerator and can be found in the refrigerated section of grocery stores.

REGULAR TOFU

Regular tofu is packed in water and sold in hard plastic containers sealed with plastic film. This type of tofu is available soft, firm, and extra-firm. Soft regular tofu works well for scrambles because it has a soft, eggy texture with a bit more bite than silken tofu. Firm regular tofu also makes a great scramble and can be easily cubed, crumbled, or cut into various shapes. Extra-firm regular tofu is the best kind for steaks. When properly prepared, it's chewy and has a meaty texture that many people like. Super-firm regular tofu, which is more difficult to find, comes shrink-wrapped in plastic. It's firm enough to stand up to any grill.

If you're unable to find super-firm regular tofu, you can press firm or extra-firm regular tofu to rid it of excess water. Just wrap the block of tofu in a clean kitchen towel to absorb the moisture and lay something flat and heavy on top of it, such as a heavy pan or skillet. The item should be heavy enough to press the moisture out but not so heavy that the tofu is crushed or crumbles. Let the tofu rest for thirty minutes. When you unwrap it, you'll be shocked at the amount of water that block of tofu was holding! There are fancy gadgets you can buy to press tofu, and if that's your thing, by all means get one. But a cast iron skillet and a kitchen towel are less expensive and work just as well.

TEMPEH

Tempeh originated in Indonesia. Like its cousin, tofu, tempeh is made from soybeans and is often used in recipes to replace meat. Although tempeh and tofu function similarly in recipes, their taste and texture differ. Tempeh is made with fermented whole soybeans that are pressed into a "cake." Tempeh is denser than even the firmest tofu and also has more texture from the whole beans. As a result, tempeh has more protein, fiber, and other nutrients than tofu, along with a lot more flavor. The flavor of tempeh has been described as nutty or earthy, and it meshes quite well with a wide range of sauces and marinades.

BREAKFAST IS USUALLY DEFINED AS the first meal of the day, typically eaten in the morning. But many people like to have breakfast for dinner (aka "brinner"). Whether you like sweet or savory breakfast foods or prefer your pancakes at midnight, you'll find something in this chapter that whispers sweet nothings in your ear. For most mornings at Casa de Herbivore, we stick with the quickies: toast, granola with fruit, or oatmeal. On weekends we often indulge in a scramble or pancakes. But I am fanatical about having leftovers for breakfast and generally lean toward savory options, so you might very well find me rooting through the fridge for remnants of previous meals for my breakfast.

Breakfast

Savory Breakfast Grain Bowl, Page 40

APPLES AND PEANUT BUTTER are a magical combo. Toss them in a blender with some complementary flavorings and you'll have a smoothie that tastes like dessert. The healthy blend of protein and carbohydrates makes this an excellent drink before or after exercising.

Apple & Peanut Butter Smoothie

PUT ALL THE ingredients in a blender and process on high speed until smooth.

Variation: Replace the peanut butter with 3 tablespoons of almond butter, cashew butter, sunflower seed butter, or whatever nut butter you're nuts about.

Per serving: 393 calories, 10 g protein, 14 g fat (2 g sat), 59 g carbohydrates, 46 mg sodium, 191 mg calcium, 8 g fiber

MAKES 2 LARGE SERVINGS

3 small apples, cored and chopped (peeling optional)

2 cups ice (about 10 cubes)

1½ frozen bananas, broken into pieces

¾ cup plain or vanilla nondairy milk

3 tablespoons unsalted natural peanut butter

1 tablespoon maple syrup

1 teaspoon vanilla extract

1 teaspoon light molasses

½ teaspoon ground cinnamon

AT CASA DE HERBIVORE, Josh is the smoothie master. In the summertime, mint grows like crazy all around the yard, so we add lots of fresh mint to all our smoothies and salads. This combination is sweet and creamy from the banana and pear, and it has a lovely green hue, compliments of the kale and mint.

Minty Kale-Pear Smoothie

MAKES 2 LARGE SERVINGS

4 cups stemmed and coarsely torn kale leaves, packed

2 cups ice (about 10 cubes)

2 pears, cored and chopped (peeling optional)

2 frozen bananas

1½ cups plain or vanilla nondairy milk

¼ cup fresh mint leaves, lightly packed, or ¼ teaspoon mint extract

2 tablespoons light molasses

1 teaspoon vanilla extract

PUT ALL THE ingredients in a blender and process on high speed until smooth.

Tip: It's best to use a high-powered blender when processing kale. If you don't have one, replace the kale with 2 cups of baby spinach, packed.

Per serving: 435 calories, 19 g protein, 4 g fat (1 g sat), 92 g carbohydrates, 166 mg sodium, 656 mg calcium, 18 g fiber

THIS QUICK BREAKFAST is so simple that it hardly seems like a recipe, yet I believe no Herbivore's life should be without it. Use whichever nut butter and bread your heart desires.

Nut Butter & Bacon Toast

SPREAD THE TOAST with the nut butter. Top with the Better-than-Bacon Crumbles or Strips and serve.

Tip: For a fancier presentation, cut the toast on a diagonal.

Per serving: 561 calories, 30 g protein, 33 g fat (7 g sat), 39 g carbohydrates, 754 mg sodium, 203 mg calcium, 5 g fiber

MAKES 2 SERVINGS

2 slices whole-grain or gluten-free bread, toasted
2 tablespoons nut butter
1 recipe Better-than-Bacon Crumbles or Strips (page 77), ½ cup Coconut Flakes Better-than-Bacon (page 69), or 6 strips vegan bacon, cooked

GRANOLA IS A VERY simple food that, unfortunately, has been ruined by the food industry. Oats mixed with nuts and seeds should not have as much sugar as a candy bar or as much oil as a lava lamp. It also shouldn't cost eight dollars a pound. (Clearly, I have a lot of issues with mass-produced granola!) The solution? Make your own! This mixture contains delicious foods from the Northwest: hazelnuts, cherries, and cranberries.

Northwest Granola

MAKES 5 CUPS

3 cups old-fashioned rolled oats
¾ cup finely chopped raw hazelnuts
¼ cup raw sunflower seeds, whole or chopped
2 tablespoons flax meal
1 teaspoon salt
½ teaspoon ground cinnamon
¼ cup maple syrup
¼ cup well-mashed banana
2 tablespoons brown sugar
2 tablespoons coconut oil, melted
2 teaspoons vanilla extract
Zest of 1 orange
½ cup unsweetened dried cherries, coarsely chopped
½ cup unsweetened dried cranberries

PREHEAT THE OVEN to 300 degrees F. Line a rimmed baking sheet with parchment paper.

Put the oats, hazelnuts, sunflower seeds, flax meal, salt, and cinnamon in a large bowl and stir to combine. Put the maple syrup, banana, brown sugar, coconut oil, vanilla extract, and orange zest in a small bowl and stir until well combined. Pour over the oat mixture and stir with a silicone spatula until evenly distributed. Spoon the mixture into the lined pan, spreading it evenly.

Bake for 30 minutes. Remove from the oven and stir. Spread the mixture out again and bake for 20 minutes longer, until crispy and brown. It should smell incredible. Let cool for 10 to 15 minutes, then stir in the cherries and cranberries. Let cool completely. Store in tightly sealed glass jars or storage containers at room temperature.

Per cup: 632 calories, 13 g protein, 36 g fat (8 g sat), 74 g carbohydrates, 499 mg sodium, 73 mg calcium, 12 g fiber

I LOVE BISCUITS, but I don't like to use large amounts of shortening, oil, or vegan butter to make them. That just seems so decadent and heart stopping. Still, I love biscuits! You see the quandary here, don't you? Then I discovered that cashew cream or soy creamer makes a perfectly light and flaky biscuit without a cup of fat. Biscuits every day, anyone?

Cream Biscuits

MAKES 8 BISCUITS

1 cup white whole wheat flour
1 cup unbleached all-purpose
    flour, plus more for kneading
2 teaspoons baking powder
½ teaspoon salt
½ cup Cashew Cream (page 56)
    plus ½ cup water, or 1 cup
    unflavored soy creamer

PREHEAT THE OVEN to 425 degrees F. Line a baking sheet with parchment paper or mist with cooking spray.

Put the flour, baking powder, and salt in a large bowl and stir to combine. Put the Cashew Cream and water in a small bowl and stir until smooth and well combined. Pour into the flour mixture and stir to form a dough.

Sprinkle a clean surface with a small amount of flour. Turn the dough out onto the floured surface and gently knead about ten times. Sprinkle with additional flour as necessary to keep the dough from sticking. Divide the dough into eight equal balls. Pat out each ball to make a ¾-inch-thick round. Arrange on the lined baking sheet about two inches apart. Bake for about 15 minutes, until lightly golden.

Variation: For larger biscuits, divide the dough into four balls and bake for 20 minutes.

Per biscuit: 139 calories, 5 g protein, 3 g fat (1 g sat), 25 g carbohydrates, 215 mg sodium, 48 mg calcium, 2 g fiber

MAYBE IT'S BECAUSE I'm not from the South, but I didn't grow up eating biscuits and gravy. After I became vegan, however, I was shown the light. Almonds and soy milk make a rich, creamy gravy, and sage and pepper add the perfect seasonings. The result? A smooth, savory gravy to top a fluffy biscuit in the morning or anytime. As a bonus, it's quick to make and almost impossible to mess up.

Sage Gravy

PUT THE ALMOND MEAL, flour, nutritional yeast, sage, garlic granules, and pepper in a medium saucepan and whisk to combine. Whisk in the water, milk, and tamari until smooth, making sure to incorporate the flour from the sides of the saucepan. Bring to a boil over medium heat, whisking frequently. Decrease the heat to medium and simmer, whisking frequently, until thick and smooth, about 10 minutes. Whisk in additional pepper to taste if desired. Whisk in the lemon juice just before serving.

Per ¼ cup: 47 calories, 2 g protein, 2 g fat (0.1 g sat), 4 g carbohydrates, 80 mg sodium, 64 mg calcium, 1 g fiber

MAKES 2 CUPS

¼ cup almond meal or almond flour
¼ cup unbleached all-purpose flour, white whole wheat flour, or spelt flour
2 tablespoons nutritional yeast flakes
2 teaspoons rubbed sage
1 teaspoon garlic granules
¼ teaspoon freshly ground pepper, plus more if desired
1 cup water
1 cup unsweetened nondairy milk
2 teaspoons reduced-sodium tamari
½ teaspoon lemon juice

Go-To Greens, Page 118

WE LIKE TO PACK our tofu scramble with whatever veggies are in the fridge. The more the better—we're vegan, after all! But back when we ate eggs, there were never veggies in our scramble. So, on behalf of newbies, this recipe has nary a vegetable. Instead, the focus is on cooking tofu into a delicious breakfast, with some crispy parts and some soft parts, just the way a scramble should be. Serve it with toast or an English muffin and a side of fruit.

Herbivore's Tofu Scramble

PUT THE NUTRITIONAL yeast, garlic granules, onion granules, salt, and turmeric in a small bowl and stir to combine. Set aside.

Put the oil in a medium skillet (cast iron if you have one) and tilt the skillet to spread it evenly. Alternatively, mist the skillet with cooking spray. Heat over medium heat. When hot, add the tofu and spread it evenly in the pan. Now, here's what to do: NOTHING. The secret is to leave the tofu alone and let the hot pan do the work so the tofu can brown. Cook, stirring only occasionally, until dry looking and parts are crispy, about 10 minutes. Sprinkle the nutritional yeast mixture over the the tofu, pour the water in the center, and stir until evenly distributed. Cover and remove from the heat. Keep covered until ready to serve. Season with pepper to taste.

Per serving: 194 calories, 19 g protein, 12 g fat (2 g sat), 4 g carbohydrates, 305 mg sodium, 131 mg calcium, 1 g fiber

MAKES 4 SERVINGS

2 tablespoons nutritional yeast flakes
1 teaspoon garlic granules
1 teaspoon onion granules
$\frac{1}{2}$ teaspoon salt
$\frac{1}{8}$ teaspoon ground turmeric
1 teaspoon olive oil
1 package (1 pound) firm or extra-firm tofu, patted dry and crumbled
2 tablespoons water
Freshly ground pepper

SOUK MEANS "MARKET" in Arabic, and this scramble is full of everyday market ingredients that come together to create a delicious breakfast infused with Middle Eastern flavor. Josh and I decided to get married during a trip to Lebanon, so anything Arabic is special to us. This recipe is in no way authentic, because we never ate tofu in Lebanon, but who's checking? Serve it with pita bread if you want to tie in the theme.

Souk Scramble

MAKES 4 SERVINGS

2 tablespoons nutritional yeast flakes
1 teaspoon garlic granules
1 teaspoon onion granules
½ teaspoon dried basil
½ teaspoon dried thyme
¼ teaspoon salt
⅛ teaspoon ground turmeric
2 tablespoons water
1 tablespoon reduced-sodium tamari
1 teaspoon olive oil
1 package (1 pound) firm or extra-firm tofu, patted dry and crumbled
2 cups chopped spinach, lightly packed
⅓ cup chopped kalamata olives
1 cup chopped tomato
Freshly ground pepper

PUT THE NUTRITIONAL yeast, garlic granules, onion granules, basil, thyme, salt, and turmeric in a small bowl and stir to combine. Put the water and tamari in another small bowl or measuring cup. Set both bowls aside.

Put the oil in a medium skillet (cast iron if you have one) and tilt the skillet to spread it evenly. Alternatively, mist the skillet with cooking spray. Heat over medium heat. When hot, add the tofu and spread it evenly in the pan. Now, here's what to do: NOTHING. The secret is to leave the tofu alone and let the hot pan do the work so the tofu can brown. Cook, stirring only occasionally, until dry looking and parts are crispy, about 10 minutes. Sprinkle the nutritional yeast mixture over the the tofu and stir until evenly distributed. Stir in the spinach and olives. Cover and cook for 2 minutes, until the spinach is wilted. Add the tamari mixture and stir to combine. Add the tomato and remove from the heat. Keep covered until ready to serve. Season with pepper to taste.

Per serving: 286 calories, 22 g protein, 21 g fat (3 g sat), 12 g carbohydrates, 667 mg sodium, 204 mg calcium, 4 g fiber

CABBAGE IS A LOT like tofu—it gets no respect. Somewhere I read that if there is a nuclear war, cabbage would be a good food to seek out because the outer leaves act as a barrier and protect the inner leaves. Amazing, huh? More applicable here, cabbage is inexpensive, yummy, nutritious, and filling, which is exactly what I need in the morning. Fennel and mustard are cabbage's best friends, so naturally they make an appearance.

Survival Scramble

PUT THE TAMARI, mustard, agave nectar, fennel seeds, and turmeric in a small bowl and stir to combine. Set aside.

Heat the oil in a large skillet (cast iron if you have one) over medium heat. Alternatively, mist the skillet with cooking spray. When hot, add the onion and cook, stirring frequently, for 3 minutes. Stir in the potato, cover, and cook for 7 to 10 minutes. Let cook undisturbed, as this will help the potato brown. Then stir, cover, and cook undisturbed for 7 minutes longer. If the potato is sticking or burning, decrease the heat to medium-low.

Add the tofu, cabbage, and tamari mixture and stir well to combine. Cook, stirring once or twice, for 8 minutes. Add 2 to 3 teaspoons of water if the mixture becomes too dry or sticks to the skillet. Season with pepper to taste. Sprinkle the bell pepper over the scramble just before serving.

Per serving: 262 calories, 20 g protein, 14 g fat (3 g sat), 15 g carbohydrates, 411 mg sodium, 321 mg calcium, 2 g fiber

MAKES 4 SERVINGS

2 tablespoons reduced-sodium tamari

1 tablespoon whole-grain mustard

1 teaspoon agave nectar or maple syrup

$\frac{1}{2}$ teaspoon whole fennel seeds, crushed or coarsely ground

$\frac{1}{8}$ teaspoon ground turmeric

1 tablespoon olive oil

$\frac{1}{2}$ cup chopped yellow onion

1 cup unpeeled chopped white potato

1 package (1 pound) firm or extra-firm tofu, patted dry and crumbled

1 cup finely chopped green cabbage

Freshly ground black pepper

$\frac{1}{3}$ cup finely diced red bell pepper

THE WORD "RANCH" brings many images to mind. There's ranch dressing, the Wild West with cowboys and vast expanses of land, and ranch-style homes. This scramble is my tribute to all of these. Be traditional and eat this scramble with a Cream Biscuit (page 22). Yee-haw!

Ranch Scramble

PUT THE NUTRITIONAL yeast, dill weed, lemon pepper, salt, and turmeric in a small bowl and stir to combine. Put the water and tamari in another small bowl or measuring cup. Set both bowls aside.

Put the oil in a medium skillet (cast iron if you have one) and tilt the skillet to spread it evenly. Alternatively, mist the skillet with cooking spray. Heat over medium heat. When hot, add the tofu and spread it evenly in the pan. Now, here's what to do: NOTHING. The secret is to leave the tofu alone and let the hot pan do the work so the tofu can brown. Cook, stirring only occasionally, until dry looking and parts are crispy, about 10 minutes.

Add the broccoli, cover, and let steam until bright green, about 4 minutes. Sprinkle the nutritional yeast mixture over the the tofu and stir until evenly distributed. Add the tamari mixture and stir to combine. Stir in the tomato, scallions, and parsley. Put 1 tablespoon of the sour cream in each quadrant of the mixture. Cover and remove from the heat. The sour cream will melt into the scramble. Keep covered until ready to serve.

Per serving: 263 calories, 21 g protein, 20 g fat (4 g sat), 11 g carbohydrates, 364 mg sodium, 164 mg calcium, 3 g fiber

MAKES 4 SERVINGS

2 tablespoons nutritional yeast flakes
$\frac{1}{2}$ teaspoon dried dill weed
$\frac{1}{2}$ teaspoon lemon pepper
$\frac{1}{4}$ teaspoon salt
$\frac{1}{8}$ teaspoon ground turmeric
2 tablespoons water
1 tablespoon reduced-sodium tamari
1 teaspoon olive oil
1 package (1 pound) firm or extra-firm tofu, patted dry and crumbled
1 cup bite-sized broccoli florets
$\frac{1}{2}$ cup chopped tomato
$\frac{1}{3}$ cup sliced scallions
2 tablespoons chopped fresh parsley, or 2 teaspoons dried
$\frac{1}{4}$ cup vegan sour cream

WE LOVE TO MAKE these tacos when we have leftover Crushed and Crispy Potatoes (page 106), but it's almost just as fast to make them with freshly chopped potatoes, as described here. The combination of store-bought vegan sausage, fennel, and tofu, all wrapped up in a tortilla and served with avocado and salsa, pulls together the best of both traditional diner breakfasts and breakfast tacos.

Diner Breakfast Tacos

MAKES 8 TACOS, 4 SERVINGS

Taco Filling

2 tablespoons olive oil
1 cup finely diced onion
2 cups finely diced potatoes
4 vegan sausage patties, cut into bite-sized pieces
⅓ cup crumbled firm or extra-firm tofu
½ teaspoon whole fennel seeds, crushed or coarsely ground
⅛ teaspoon ground turmeric
3 cups chopped spinach, lightly packed
Salt
Freshly ground black pepper

Tortillas, Cheese, and Condiments

8 (8-inch) flour tortillas
½ cup shredded vegan cheese
1 avocado, sliced
Salsa, pico de gallo, or ketchup
Vegan sour cream (optional)

TO MAKE THE FILLING, heat the oil in a large skillet (cast iron if you have one) over medium heat. Add the onion and cook, stirring frequently, for 3 minutes. Stir in the potatoes, cover, and cook for 7 to 10 minutes. Let cook undisturbed, as this will help the potatoes brown. Then stir, cover, and cook undisturbed for 7 minutes longer. If the potatoes are sticking or burning, decrease the heat to medium-low.

Position an oven rack close to the broiler and preheat the broiler.

Stir the sausage, tofu, fennel, and turmeric into the potato mixture. Cook for 3 minutes, stirring occasionally. Decrease the heat to low and add the spinach. Cook, stirring occasionally, until the spinach is wilted, about 3 minutes. Season with salt and pepper to taste.

Arrange the tortillas on a baking sheet (it's okay if they hang off the edge of the sheet). Sprinkle the cheese evenly over each tortilla. Broil for about 2 minutes, until the cheese is melted and the tortilla is hot. Watch closely so the tortillas don't burn.

To serve, put ⅓ cup of the filling on each tortilla over the cheese and fold in half. Pass the avocado, salsa, and optional sour cream at the table.

Per taco: 314 calories, 13 g protein, 14g fat (3 g sat), 37 g carbohydrates, 573 mg sodium, 156 mg calcium, 5 g fiber

Note: Analysis doesn't include salt, freshly ground pepper, salsa, pico de gallo, or ketchup to taste.

THE NEW FARM VEGETARIAN COOKBOOK, first published in 1975, is the classic hippy vegetarian cookbook. An entire generation of vegans and vegetarians can picture the cover as soon as they hear the name. We still sell the book in our store today! This is one of our favorite recipes, located on the page our book falls open to whenever we set it down. I think just about every vegan pancake recipe written since then is an adaptation of The Farm's recipe, so why mess around with perfection? Here it is. Peace.

The Farm Pancakes

MAKES 10 PANCAKES

PREHEAT THE OVEN to 200 degrees F. Put a large ovenproof plate on a rack to keep the pancakes hot while you make the whole batch.

Put the flour, sugar, baking powder, and salt in a large bowl and whisk to combine. Put the milk and oil in a large measuring cup. Make a well in the middle of the dry ingredients, pour in the milk mixture, and stir with a silicone spatula until just combined (a few small lumps are fine). If the batter is overmixed, the pancakes will be thin and tough. Let the batter rest for 5 minutes.

Mist a large skillet (cast iron if you have one) or smooth griddle with cooking spray and heat over medium heat. When hot, add the batter in batches (depending on the size of the skillet), using $\frac{1}{4}$ cup per pancake. Cook until browned on the bottom and bubbles appear on the top, about 3 minutes. Flip and cook until browned on the other side, 1 to 2 minutes. Transfer to the plate in the oven to keep warm while you make the rest of the pancakes.

Tip: If you use whole wheat flour, add 2 additional tablespoons of nondairy milk.

Variation: Add 1 teaspoon of vanilla extract to the milk and oil before stirring into the batter. Divine!

Serving suggestion: Serve the pancakes with maple syrup, agave nectar, fresh fruit, nut butter, or any of the other usual suspects in the pancake-eating world.

- $1\frac{1}{4}$ cups all-purpose unbleached flour or whole wheat flour (see tip)
- 2 tablespoons sugar
- 2 teaspoons baking powder
- $\frac{1}{2}$ teaspoon salt
- $1\frac{1}{4}$ cups plain nondairy milk
- 2 tablespoons vegetable oil

Per pancake: 101 calories, 2 g protein, 3 g fat (1 g sat), 15 g carbohydrates, 74 mg sodium, 71 mg calcium, 1 g fiber

THERE'S A LITTLE AGRICULTURAL oasis right outside of Portland called Sauvie Island. It's where everyone goes in the fall to visit the pumpkin patches or get lost in a corn maze. Summer officially starts when the island's strawberries are finally ripe and ready for picking. We make these pancakes with fresh-picked berries in June and July, and we use our stash of frozen berries during the dreary winter months, when we dream about the sunny summer days to come.

Sauvie Island Strawberry Pancakes

PREHEAT THE OVEN to 200 degrees F. Put a large ovenproof plate on a rack to keep the pancakes hot while you make the whole batch.

Zest the lemon (you should have about 1 tablespoon of zest) and then extract the juice from half of the lemon (store the other half in the fridge for another use). Set the zest aside.

Pour the milk in a large measuring cup. Stir in the lemon juice (this will make vegan buttermilk) and set aside to curdle, about 5 minutes. Add the oil, vanilla extract, and reserved lemon zest and stir to combine.

Put the flour, cornmeal, sugar, baking powder, baking soda, and salt in a large bowl and whisk to combine. Make a well in the middle of the dry ingredients, pour in the milk mixture, and stir with a silicone spatula. Stir until the ingredients are just combined (a few small lumps are fine). If the batter is overmixed, the pancakes will be thin and tough. Stir in the strawberries. Let the batter rest for 5 minutes.

Mist a large skillet (cast iron if you have one) or smooth griddle with cooking spray and heat over medium heat. When hot, add the batter in batches (depending on the size of the skillet), using ⅓ cup per pancake. Cook until browned on the bottom and bubbles appear on the top, about 3 minutes. Flip and cook until browned on the other side, 1 to 2 minutes. Transfer to the plate in the oven to keep warm while you make the rest of the pancakes.

Per pancake: 106 calories, 3 g protein, 2 g fat (0.2 g sat), 20 g carbohydrates, 3 mg sodium, 74 mg calcium, 3 g fiber

MAKES 12 PANCAKES

1 lemon
1 cup plain or vanilla nondairy milk
1 tablespoon vegetable oil
1 teaspoon vanilla extract
1 cup white whole wheat flour
1 cup cornmeal
2 tablespoons sugar
1 teaspoon baking powder
½ teaspoon baking soda
½ teaspoon salt
2 cups chopped strawberries

MY MOTHER NEVER liked oatmeal until I made this recipe for her on a visit home. I forever changed her opinion because this oatmeal is so incredibly special and awesome. We make this at least once a week. Baked oatmeal has a crisp top and bottom and a soft center. The consistency falls somewhere between regular cooked oatmeal and a breakfast bar.

Mama Herbivore's Oatmeal

MAKES 6 SERVINGS

2 cups old-fashioned rolled oats
⅓ cup finely ground almonds or other nuts
2 tablespoons sugar
1 teaspoon baking powder
1 teaspoon ground cinnamon
½ teaspoon salt
¼ teaspoon grated nutmeg
2 large bananas, sliced
2¼ cups plain or vanilla nondairy milk
2 teaspoons vanilla extract
1 cup fresh or frozen berries (any kind)

PREHEAT THE OVEN to 375 degrees F. Mist an 8-inch square baking pan with cooking spray.

Put the oats, almonds, sugar, baking powder, cinnamon, salt, and nutmeg in a large bowl and stir to combine.

Arrange the bananas in the baking dish; it's okay if they overlap. Sprinkle the oat mixture evenly over the bananas. Put the milk and vanilla extract in the bowl you used for the dry ingredients (why dirty another bowl?) and stir to combine. Slowly pour over the oat mixture, evenly saturating it. The liquid should rise up over the oat mixture. Scatter the berries evenly over the top. Bake for 35 minutes. Let cool for 5 minutes before serving.

Tip: The oatmeal will become firmer the longer it sits. If you choose to make it in advance, you can slice it into bars before serving. Preheat the oven to 300 degrees F and line a baking sheet with parchment paper. Put the bars on the lined baking sheet and warm them in the oven for about 5 minutes.

Per serving: 242 calories, 4 g protein, 7 g fat (1 g sat), 21 g carbohydrates, 280 mg sodium, 141 mg calcium, 3 g fiber

THIS GLUTEN-FREE recipe was inspired by cereal bars I ate during my college years, except these are made with pronounceable ingredients. Bake these up for a perfect to-go breakfast, a lunch-box snack, or a treat with coffee at your desk.

Oat-Berry Breakfast Bars

PREHEAT THE OVEN to 350 degrees F. Line an 8-inch square baking pan with waxed paper or parchment paper (the paper should extend over the sides a bit) and press it in as best as possible.

Put the oats, flour, sugar, flax meal, baking powder, salt, and cinnamon in a large bowl. Add the banana, milk, oil, and vanilla extract and mix well. Spread half the oat mixture evenly in the prepared baking dish. This will be the top layer of the bars. Lift out using the waxed paper and set aside.

Mist the baking pan with cooking spray and evenly spread the remaining oat mixture in the pan. Spread the berries evenly over the oat mixture in the pan. Carefully invert the oat mixture that's on the waxed paper and place it on top of the fruit. Make sure that all the fruit is covered (use your fingers to spread it out where necessary). Bake for 30 minutes. Cool completely before slicing into 6 bars.

Tip: For the berries, try blueberries, halved raspberries, or sliced strawberries.

Per bar: 207 calories, 4 g protein, 6 g fat (1 g sat), 36 g carbohydrates, 76 mg sodium, 64 mg calcium, 4 g fiber

MAKES 6 SERVINGS

1½ cups old-fashioned rolled oats
¾ cup brown rice flour
½ cup sugar
¼ cup flax meal
1 teaspoon baking powder
½ teaspoon salt
½ teaspoon ground cinnamon
½ cup mashed banana
  (about 1 banana)
½ cup plain or vanilla
  nondairy milk
2 tablespoons vegetable oil
1 teaspoon vanilla extract
1 cup sliced fresh berries, or
  ¾ cup strawberry or blueberry
  preserves (enough to cover
  the bottom layer of oats)

ELVIS WAS KNOWN for his love of peanut butter and banana sandwiches, but I bet he would have loved this quesadilla too. Nut butter should be a staple in every vegan's diet. It's filling and tastes incredible. Plus, it has lots of protein, is affordable, and is available everywhere. Use whichever kind of nut butter you prefer in this recipe. If you add some Better-than-Bacon Coconut Flakes, Elvis just might join you for breakfast.

Elvis Quesadilla with Maple-Yogurt Drizzle

MAKES 1 QUESADILLA, 1 SERVING

2 tablespoons unsalted natural peanut butter or other nut butter
1 (10-inch) whole-grain tortilla
½ banana
Dash ground cinnamon
¼ cup Better-than-Bacon Coconut Flakes (page 69; optional)
¼ cup plain or vanilla vegan yogurt
1 tablespoon maple syrup

MIST A SKILLET or smooth griddle lightly with cooking spray and heat over medium heat. Spread the peanut butter on half the tortilla and put the banana on the other half. Sprinkle the cinnamon over the banana, then sprinkle with the optional Better-than-Bacon. Lay the tortilla in the hot skillet. Let it heat for a moment before folding it over (that will keep the tortilla from tearing). Cook until crispy on the bottom, about 4 minutes. Carefully turn over and cook until the other side is crispy, 3 to 4 minutes.

While the quesadilla is cooking, put the yogurt and maple syrup in a small bowl and whisk until evenly combined.

To serve, cut the quesadilla into four equal pieces. Drizzle the yogurt mixture over the top or serve it on the side for dipping.

Per serving: 484 calories, 13 g protein, 21 g fat (5 g sat), 65 g carbohydrates, 468 mg sodium, 20 mg calcium, 8 g fiber

JUST BECAUSE I'M vegan doesn't mean I don't love meat and cheese. I just like meat and cheese that comes from plants. This knock-off fast-food sandwich comes together more slowly than a drive-through's version, but that's a small price to pay for cruelty-free food. If you have leftover biscuits lounging around your kitchen, you can make these lickety-split. Since you're vegan now, it's customary to have a little green with most meals. Good morning, spinach!

Sausage Biscuit Breakfast Sandwiches

MIST A LARGE skillet or smooth griddle lightly with cooking spray and heat over medium heat. When hot, put the sausage patties in the skillet and cook according to the package directions. About 3 minutes before the patties are done cooking, scoot the patties to one side of the skillet and put the spinach in the other side. Let the spinach cook until wilted, about 1 minute.

While the spinach is cooking, cut the cheese slices in half. Put half of one of the biscuits in the skillet (cut-side up), top with half a cheese slice, then a sausage patty, then another half a cheese slice, then one-quarter of the spinach. Put the other biscuit half cut-side down in the skillet so it toasts and gets warm, then put it on top of the sandwich. Repeat with all the remaining biscuits, cheese, sausage patties, and spinach until four sandwiches are assembled and in the skillet. Cover the skillet so the cheese will melt. Serve hot.

Per sandwich: 305 calories, 18 g protein, 11 g fat (4 g sat), 37 g carbohydrates, 595 mg sodium, 123 mg calcium, 5 g fiber

MAKES 4 SANDWICHES

4 vegan sausage patties
2 cups chopped spinach
4 slices vegan cheese
4 large Cream Biscuits (see variation, page 22), halved

HERE'S A GREAT USE for leftover quinoa, rice, or farro, or a good reason to cook up a pot the night before so you can throw this together in the morning while drinking your coffee. This recipe is totally adaptable: use leftover kale salad instead of spinach, add broccoli or leftover roasted vegetables, or try a combination of grains. The key is the grain, vegetable, nut, and fruit combo with the simple, savory dressing.

Savory Breakfast Grain Bowl

PUT THE SPINACH in a microwave-safe bowl and cover with the grain. Heat on high until the grain is steaming (the time will depend on your microwave). Once the grain is hot, add the cranberries, walnuts, oil, nutritional yeast, and tamari and mix well. Alternatively, put the spinach and grain in a medium saucepan and add 1 to 2 tablespoons of water. Cover and heat over medium heat, stirring occasionally, until hot, about 2 minutes. Transfer to a small bowl. Add the cranberries, walnuts, oil, nutritional yeast, and tamari and mix well.

Variation: Top with diced avocado just before serving.

Per serving: 655 calories, 17 g protein, 26 g fat (2 g sat), 91 g carbohydrates, 708 mg sodium, 119 mg calcium, 9 g fiber

MAKES 1 SERVING

1 cup chopped baby spinach, lightly packed

1½ cups cooked grain

2 tablespoons dried cranberries, raisins, chopped dried apricots, or dried cherries

2 tablespoons chopped walnuts, almonds, hemp seeds, or other nuts or seeds

1 tablespoon flax, walnut, or olive oil

1 tablespoon nutritional yeast flakes or Yellow Rose Parmesan (page 50)

2 teaspoons reduced-sodium tamari

MOST PEOPLE KEEP CERTAIN foods in the fridge at all times and have favorite dishes, ingredients, and preparations that are done so frequently they've basically become muscle memory. That's what the recipes in this section are for us in the Herbivore kitchen: dressings, sauces, and simple vegan alternatives for meat and dairy favorites that we use regularly. Everybody needs a great recipe for peanut sauce, pesto, red sauce, and creamy dressing that can be whipped up in minutes. So here you go! There is also a little meet and greet with the great vegan proteins: seitan, tofu, and tempeh. These three amigos will cause you to pause and joyfully reconsider what it means for a dish to be "meaty."

Basics & Staples

Don't-Be-Blue Cheese Dressing, Page 44   Red Bird Marinara, Page 57   Peanut-Hoisin Sauce, Page 62   Tahini Sauce, Page 45

THIS IS THE SALAD dressing we use almost every day. We don't make it in advance and keep it in the fridge; we just mix it right in the salad bowl before we add the salad items. We generally just eyeball the dressing ingredients rather than measure; it fits our style. You can use the recipe as written, or double it, or halve it, or experiment with dressing your salad right in the bowl as we do. Use flax, olive, avocado, grape seed, or walnut oil and see which you prefer. We like to switch it up a bit, but we always use nutritional yeast, because that's what makes it so darned special.

Herbivore House Dressing

MAKES 1 CUP

½ cup vegetable oil
⅓ cup reduced-sodium tamari
⅓ cup nutritional yeast flakes
Freshly ground pepper

PUT THE OIL, tamari, and nutritional yeast in a jar. Seal tightly and shake until the dressing is emulsified. Season with pepper to taste and shake again until incorporated. Alternatively, whisk the ingredients in a small bowl or process them in a blender.

Tip: If you opt to dress the salad in the bowl, just sprinkle the oil, tamari, and nutritional yeast over the veggies, grind some pepper on top, and toss. You can adjust the flavors more easily if you start with less oil and tamari. You can always add more oil and tamari, but you can't remove them!

Per 2 tablespoons: 147 calories, 3 g protein, 14 g fat (1 g sat), 2 g carbohydrates, 473 mg sodium, 13 mg calcium, 1 g fiber

I GREW UP USING straight mayo as a salad dressing, so my love of creamy dressings runs wide and deep. This recipe is similar to the ranch dressing many people know and love but with a delightful tarragon twist. Use it to cool off spicy food, such as Spicy Hot Tofu (page 74) or Chopped Salad with Spicy Hot Chickpeas (page 84).

Creamy Tarragon Ranch Dressing

PUT ALL THE INGREDIENTS in a small bowl and whisk until well combined. Alternatively, put all the ingredients in a jar, seal tightly, and shake until well combined.

Per 2 tablespoons: 124 calories, 0 g protein, 12 g fat (1 g sat), 1 g carbohydrates, 164 mg sodium, 13 mg calcium, 0 g fiber

MAKES 1½ CUPS

1 cup vegan mayonnaise
½ cup unsweetened
    nondairy milk
1 tablespoon dried tarragon
1 teaspoon onion granules
½ teaspoon garlic granules
¼ teaspoon salt
Pinch freshly ground
    black pepper

I'M NOT SURE HOW close this is to blue cheese dressing made with dairy products, but dang if this version doesn't scream BLUE CHEESE to me! Tossed with crunchy lettuce, served as a dip with fries, or used to cool off Curry-Barbecue Soy Curls Bowls (page 142), this dressing will make you want to have some on hand at all times. Nothin' wrong with eating a couple of spoonfuls straight out of the bowl, either.

Don't-Be-Blue Cheese Dressing

MAKES 1¼ CUPS

½ cup vegan mayonnaise
¼ cup unsweetened soy milk
¼ cup lemon juice
1 scallion, finely chopped
2 tablespoons chopped fresh
    parsley, or 1 tablespoon dried
2 tablespoons tahini
2 teaspoons yellow or
    white miso
2 teaspoons cider vinegar
1 teaspoon chopped garlic
¼ teaspoon salt
Pinch freshly ground pepper
½ cup pressed and crumbled
    firm tofu

PUT THE MAYONNAISE, soy milk, lemon juice, scallion, parsley, tahini, miso, vinegar, garlic, salt, and pepper in a medium bowl and whisk until smooth and well combined. Stir in the tofu until evenly distributed. Cover and chill in the refrigerator for 30 minutes before using.

Per 2 tablespoons: 88 calories, 2 g protein, 8 g fat (1 g sat), 1 g carbohydrates, 164 mg sodium, 31 mg calcium, 1 g fiber

IF THIS IS YOUR introduction to tahini, you'll probably want to start off with a small jar of it. If you're like us and use this sauce on salads, noodles, and rice dishes, it won't be long before you're buying a five-pound jug. Tahini sauce is kind of like lemon juice or salt; there isn't much that it doesn't go with.

Tahini Sauce

PUT ALL THE INGREDIENTS in a food processor or blender and process until smooth.

Tip: Like all natural nut butters, tahini needs to be stirred well to incorporate the oil prior to use.

Per 2 tablespoons: 62 calories, 2 g protein, 5 g fat (1 g sat), 2 g carbohydrates, 122 mg sodium, 1 mg calcium, 1 g fiber

MAKES 1½ CUPS

1 cup water
½ cup tahini
¼ cup lemon juice
1 tablespoon chopped garlic
½ teaspoon salt

So Faux Feta, Page 47

Popeye Pesto, Page 48

Tofu Ricotta, Page 49

Yellow Rose Parmesan, Page 50

JOSH AND I WERE GIVEN *How It All Vegan!* by Sarah Kramer when we moved in together. That book ignited a love of vegan cooking as well as a longtime friendship with Sarah. One of our favorite recipes in that book is Faux Feta, which opened my mind to the miracles of tofu and inspired this version.

So Faux Feta

PUT THE VINEGAR, oil, water, miso, basil, salt, and oregano in a large bowl and whisk until well combined. Add the tofu and stir until well combined. Cover and refrigerate for at least 1 hour to let the flavors meld.

Per ¼ cup: 90 calories, 6 g protein, 7 g fat (1 g sat), 2 g carbohydrates, 121 mg sodium, 49 mg calcium, 0 g fiber

MAKES 3 CUPS

⅓ cup red wine vinegar
3 tablespoons olive oil
3 tablespoons water
1 tablespoon yellow or
   white miso
2 teaspoons dried basil
½ teaspoon salt
½ teaspoon dried oregano
Freshly ground black pepper
1 package (1 pound) extra-firm
   tofu, patted dry and coarsely
   crumbled or cubed

THE BRIGHT GREEN color of this spinach pesto will put a smile on your face. You'll also smile knowing that spinach is more affordable and readily available than fresh basil, which is traditionally used in pesto. The walnuts in this recipe are also much less costly than pine nuts, another standard pesto ingredient. With prewashed baby spinach, this pesto comes together so quickly it's almost ridiculous.

Popeye Pesto

MAKES 1 CUP

3 cloves garlic
1 bag (5 ounces) prewashed
   baby spinach
¼ cup nutritional yeast flakes
1 tablespoon lemon juice
½ teaspoon salt
½ cup chopped walnuts
¼ cup olive oil

PULSE THE GARLIC in a food processor until finely chopped, stopping to scrape down the work bowl with a silicone spatula as needed. Add the spinach, nutritional yeast, lemon juice, and salt. Process until the spinach is chopped and the ingredients are well combined. With the machine running, add the walnuts, then slowly drizzle in the oil. Process until well combined and the texture is just the way you like it.

Variation: If you have access to fresh basil, by all means substitute it for half or even all of the spinach.

Per 2 tablespoons: 121 calories, 3 g protein, 11 g fat (1 g sat), 3 g carbohydrates, 157 mg sodium, 27 mg calcium, 1 g fiber

THIS TOFU RICOTTA is just dreamy. Use it on pizza, as a sandwich spread, in ravioli (see Sweet Potato Ravioli with Popeye Pesto Sauce, page 124), in lasagna, as a spread for bagels or toast, or as a dip for raw or cooked vegetables. When heated, the ricotta melts into supreme deliciousness.

Tofu Ricotta

PULSE THE GARLIC in a food processor until finely chopped, stopping to scrape down the work bowl with a silicone spatula as needed. Add the tofu, nutritional yeast, miso, tahini, basil, oregano, and salt and process until the mixture is well combined and speckled with herbs. Scrape down the work bowl with a silicone spatula. With the machine running, slowly pour in the oil. The mixture should be the consistency of thick sour cream.

Per serving: 200 calories, 16 g protein, 13 g fat (2 g sat), 7 g carbohydrates, 222 mg sodium, 102 mg calcium, 1 g fiber

MAKES 6 SERVINGS

4 cloves garlic, peeled
1 package (1 pound) firm or
   extra-firm tofu, crumbled
¼ cup nutritional yeast flakes
¼ cup yellow or white miso
2 tablespoons tahini
2 teaspoons dried basil
2 teaspoons dried oregano
½ teaspoon salt
1 tablespoon olive oil

HERBIVORE PUBLISHED A fabulous cookbook in 2007 called *Yellow Rose Recipes*. Written by Joanna Vaught, the book contains recipes that are still staples in our kitchen, but we use this one more frequently than any other. This Parmesan is a wholesome food made with only plant-based ingredients. Shake it on pasta, toast, salads, quesadillas, or any dishes that would appreciate something a little cheesy and salty.

Yellow Rose Parmesan

MAKES 2 CUPS

½ cup brown rice flour
½ cup nutritional yeast flakes
½ cup raw cashews
½ cup raw walnuts
1 tablespoon garlic granules
2 teaspoons salt

PUT ALL THE INGREDIENTS in a food processor and process just until the mixture turns into fine crumbs. Don't process too long or it will become a paste! Stored in a sealed container in the refrigerator, Yellow Rose Parmesan will keep for 1 month.

Per 2 tablespoons: 73 calories, 3 g protein, 4 g fat (1 g sat), 6 g carbohydrates, 296 mg sodium, 4 mg calcium, 1 g fiber

GOOD, HONEST GUACAMOLE takes about two minutes to make, which should render store-bought guac obsolete. Guacamole should be simple and pure, containing avocado and not much else. An avocado is ready to eat when the little brown stem is easily removed from its nesting place at the top of the fruit. The fruit should be firm but have a very slight give when squeezed. We should all be eating guacamole right now. Get to it.

Guacamole

HALVE AND PIT the avocados and set one of the pits aside. Use a spoon to scrape all the avocado flesh into a medium bowl. Mash it well with a fork or the back of the spoon. Add the lime juice and salt while continuing to stir and mash. Taste and add up to 1 tablespoon of additional lime juice and up to ¼ teaspoon of additional salt as desired. The longer you mash and stir the guacamole, the creamier it will be. Put the reserved pit in the center of the guacamole and cover tightly with plastic wrap until serving time; this will help keep the avocado from turning brown.

Per ¼ cup: 162 calories, 2 g protein, 15 g fat (2 g sat), 9 g carbohydrates, 150 mg sodium, 13 mg calcium, 7 g fiber

MAKES 1 CUP

3 small or 2 large avocados
1 tablespoon lime juice, plus
    more as needed
¼ teaspoon salt, plus more
    as needed

CONFESSION: I REALLY needed a vegan cheese that would go well with Mexican-inspired dishes, but I had no idea what any of the Mexican cheeses I was reading about tasted like. It had just been too long. Cheese can serve as a cool counterbalance to hot spices, so tofu seemed like a natural choice. Of course, I included some fresh jalapeño chiles and lime juice too. Now we're ready for taco night! Join us!

Tofu Queso Fresco

PUT ALL THE INGREDIENTS in a medium bowl and mash with a fork until well combined.

Per ¼ cup: 143 calories, 13 g protein, 9 g fat (2 g sat), 3 g carbohydrates, 210 mg sodium, 89 mg calcium, 1 g fiber

MAKES 1½ CUPS

1 package (1 pound) firm or extra-firm tofu, patted dry and crumbled
3 tablespoons lime juice
2 tablespoons nutritional yeast flakes
1 tablespoon minced garlic
1 tablespoon seeded and minced jalapeño chile
1 tablespoon olive oil
½ teaspoon salt

WHEN YOU'VE PUT in the effort to make Praise Seitan Vegan Roast (page 64) or Portobello-Chickpea Wellington (page 137), you just want to sit down and eat. No fussy gravy for you! This gravy will get you to the table in a flash but doesn't compromise on flavor one little bit. It's another example of how simple vegan cuisine can be deceptively healthy.

Simple Gravy

MAKES 3 CUPS

½ cup flour (all-purpose, white whole wheat, barley, or oat flour)
½ cup nutritional yeast flakes
1 teaspoon garlic granules
1 teaspoon onion granules
3 cups no-salt-added vegetable broth
2 tablespoons reduced-sodium tamari
Freshly ground pepper

PUT THE FLOUR AND nutritional yeast in a large saucepan and toast over high heat, whisking occasionally, until lightly colored and fragrant, 5 to 8 minutes. Stir in the garlic granules and onion granules. Decrease the heat to low and slowly whisk in the broth and tamari, adding only about ½ cup of liquid at a time and whisking well after each addition to prevent the gravy from becoming lumpy. When all the liquid is incorporated, increase the heat to high and bring to a boil, whisking constantly. Decrease the heat to low, cover, and simmer for 5 minutes. Season with pepper to taste.

Per ¼ cup: 41 calories, 4 g protein, 0.2 g fat (0 g sat), 8 g carbohydrates, 129 mg sodium, 0 mg calcium, 2 g fiber

BOTTLED BARBECUE SAUCE, like most other condiments, is easily purchased. But once I started making my own, I discovered how easy it is and how much fun it can be to adapt it to my tastes. Homemade condiments also make great gifts. Just jar 'em up, make a cute label, and BAM! You're the most thoughtful person ever. We like this recipe just as it is, but the possibilities are endless, so don't be shy about trying different spices to make this your own.

Barbecue Sauce

PUT THE OIL IN a large saucepan and heat over medium heat. When hot, add the onion and cook, stirring occasionally, until soft, 8 to 10 minutes. Stir in the tomatoes, raisins, brown sugar, vinegar, Worcestershire sauce, and salt. Increase the heat to high and bring to a boil. Decrease the heat to low and simmer, stirring occasionally, for 25 minutes. Cool slightly. Transfer to a blender and process until smooth.

Curry Barbecue Sauce: Add 1 tablespoon of Indian curry powder along with the tomatoes. If you prefer a spicier sauce, add up to 1 tablespoon of additional curry powder after the sauce is blended.

Per ¼ cup: 140 calories, 2 g protein, 5 g fat (1 g sat), 25 g carbohydrates, 284 mg sodium, 17 mg calcium, 3 g fiber

MAKES 1¼ CUPS

2 tablespoons vegetable oil
1 cup chopped onion
1 can (28 ounces) no-salt-added crushed tomatoes
⅓ cup raisins
¼ cup light brown sugar
¼ cup red wine vinegar
1 tablespoon vegan Worcestershire sauce
½ teaspoon salt

IN VEGAN COOKING, raw cashews are essential for creamy, rich sauces. When soaked in water, this ordinary nut is transformed into a heavy cream that is as rich as any dairy product. It really is brilliant! You'll see Cashew Cream called for in several recipes in this book. You can also use it to replace dairy cream in any conventional recipe.

Cashew Cream

MAKES 1½ CUPS

1 cup raw cashews
½ cup water

PUT THE CASHEWS in a large glass jar or medium bowl and cover with water by 3 inches. Refrigerate for 8 to 12 hours.

Drain the cashews in a colander or sieve and rinse well. Put the cashews in a blender (a high-speed blender will work best), add the water, and process on high until smooth.

Tip: If you need Cashew Cream in a hurry and don't have time to soak the cashews, you can squeak by with this quick soak. Put the cashews in a heatproof bowl and cover with boiling water. Cover the bowl with a lid or foil to keep in the heat and let soak for 30 minutes. Drain, rinse, and proceed with the recipe as directed.

Per ¼ cup: 125 calories, 4 g protein, 10 g fat (2 g sat), 7 g carbohydrates, 3 mg sodium, 8 mg calcium, 1 g fiber

IT'S REALLY SUCH A shame that people buy jarred tomato sauce, because making homemade sauce is fast and simple and the flavor is much more spectacular. Plus, homemade sauce doesn't contain any unwanted ingredients (such as corn syrup). If you prefer a chunky sauce, use diced tomatoes; if you want a smooth sauce, process it in the blender. And if you want a sauce that's somewhere in the middle, use crushed tomatoes.

Red Bird Marinara

PUT THE OIL IN a deep saucepan and heat over medium heat. When hot, add the garlic and cook, stirring frequently, for 2 minutes, taking care that the garlic doesn't brown. Stir in the basil, oregano, thyme, salt, and red pepper flakes and cook for 1 minute. Add the tomatoes and their juice, stir to combine, and simmer for 10 minutes, stirring occasionally. Stir in the vinegar and agave nectar. Taste and add more salt if desired.

Variation: Add ¼ cup of chopped kalamata olives.

Per ½ cup: 62 calories, 1 g protein, 3 g fat (1 g sat), 8 g carbohydrates, 293 mg sodium, 56 mg calcium, 1 g fiber

MAKES 2 CUPS

1 tablespoon olive oil
2 cloves garlic, minced
1 teaspoon dried basil
1 teaspoon dried oregano
1 teaspoon dried thyme
½ teaspoon salt, plus more
    as needed
¼ teaspoon crushed red
    pepper flakes
1 can (28 ounces) no-salt-added
    diced or crushed tomatoes
    with juice
1 tablespoon balsamic vinegar
1 tablespoon agave nectar

THIS CHEESE SAUCE is a breeze to prepare and decadently indulgent. It's almost criminally good in Restaurant-Style Baked Macaroni and Cheese (page 127), but you'll also love it over steamed broccoli, grilled asparagus, or baked potatoes.

Sinner's Cheese Sauce

MAKES 3 CUPS

1 cup Cashew Cream (page 56)
1 cup no-salt-added
   vegetable broth
1 cup shredded vegan cheese
   (any kind)
½ cup nutritional yeast flakes

PUT THE CASHEW CREAM and broth in a medium saucepan. Bring to a simmer over medium heat, whisking frequently. When the mixture begins to bubble, whisk in the cheese and continue whisking until it's melted. Add the nutritional yeast and continue whisking until well blended and the sauce is hot and bubbly.

Mexican-Style Cheese Sauce: Add 1 cup of canned tomatoes with green chiles or 1 cup salsa after you whisk in the nutritional yeast.

Smoky Cheese: Add 1 teaspoon of liquid smoke after you whisk in the nutritional yeast.

Per ¼ cup: 71 calories, 4 g protein, 4 g fat (1 g sat), 5 g carbohydrates, 88 mg sodium, 2 mg calcium, 2 g fiber

SOMETIMES YOU JUST crave cheesy pasta but don't want it to be overly decadent. You're vegan now, remember? You eat lots of vegetables! This sauce is a brilliant way to get a few more vegetables into your belly while still indulging in a cheesy sauce. If you've got kids or picky eaters around, don't even tell them this sauce has cauliflower in it because they would never guess. Roasting the vegetables deepens their flavor, and blending the mixture creates a familiar color with a surprisingly cheesy taste.

Saint's Cheese Sauce

MAKES 3 CUPS

PREHEAT THE OVEN to 400 degrees F. Line a rimmed baking sheet with parchment paper.

Put the sweet potato, cauliflower, onion, and garlic in a large bowl. Add the oil and tamari and toss until evenly distributed. Transfer to the lined baking sheet. Bake for 35 minutes, until the vegetables are tender and easily pierced with a knife.

While the vegetables are roasting, melt the butter in a medium saucepan over medium heat. Whisk in the flour; the mixture will be lumpy. Continue whisking until the flour turns a shade or two darker and smells rich and fragrant, about 2 minutes. Whisk in the nutritional yeast and continue whisking for 2 minutes. The mixture will become very crumbly. Gradually whisk in the broth, adding $\frac{1}{2}$ cup at a time and whisking between additions to prevent any lumps. When each addition of broth is incorporated, the mixture will become pasty, which is your signal to add another $\frac{1}{2}$ cup of broth. When all the broth has been incorporated, pour into a blender. Add the roasted vegetables and process until smooth. Scrape down the the blender jar with a silicone spatula. Add the milk, lemon juice, and salt and process until smooth. If necessary to reheat, pour into a clean medium saucepan and heat over medium heat, whisking constantly, until hot.

1 cup peeled and diced sweet potato (about 1 medium)
3 cups cauliflower florets
$\frac{1}{2}$ cup coarsely chopped onion
4 cloves garlic, peeled and smashed
2 tablespoons olive oil
1 tablespoon reduced-sodium tamari
2 tablespoons vegan butter
2 tablespoons flour (any kind)
$\frac{1}{3}$ cup nutritional yeast flakes
1$\frac{1}{2}$ cups no-salt-added vegetable broth
$\frac{1}{2}$ cup unsweetened nondairy milk
1 teaspoon lemon juice
$\frac{3}{4}$ teaspoon teaspoon salt

Per $\frac{1}{4}$ cup: 71 calories, 3 g protein, 5 g fat (1 g sat), 6 g carbohydrates, 235 mg sodium, 17 mg calcium, 1 g fiber

JOSH AND I TOOK a much-delayed honeymoon when our daughter, Ruby, was two. The three of us packed our bathing suits and spent a week on Kauai, Hawaii. We brought a suitcase of food to keep the costs down, and purchased fresh fruits and veggies once we were there. One splurge we couldn't resist was a yummy-looking salsa that had a surprise ingredient—curry powder. For years we've made this version, our homage to Hawaii and that wonderful week in the sun.

Honeymoon Mango Salsa

PUT THE INGREDIENTS in a medium bowl in the order listed. Mix well. Let sit for 1 hour before serving so the flavors can blend.

Variation: Replace the mango with 2 cups of chopped fresh or frozen papaya.

Per ¼ cup: 41 calories, 1 g protein, 0 g fat (0 g sat), 10 g carbohydrates, 86 mg sodium, 14 mg calcium, 1 g fiber

MAKES 2 CUPS

2 cups chopped fresh or
   frozen mango
½ cup finely chopped red onion
2 garlic cloves, minced
1 tablespoon minced
   fresh ginger
¼ cup chopped fresh cilantro
1 tablespoon rice vinegar
1 tablespoon lemon juice
¼ teaspoon curry powder
¼ teaspoon salt

OVER THE YEARS I've made a lot of different peanut sauces, and honestly, I love them all. But this one is the one. Perfectly peanutty, slightly spicy and sweet, and a hit with everyone (kids and grown-ups alike). Make it as spicy or mild as you like by adding more or less sriracha sauce.

Peanut-Hoisin Sauce

MAKES 1 CUP

½ cup unsweetened, unsalted natural peanut butter
¼ cup hoisin sauce
1 teaspoon sriracha sauce, plus more if desired
1¼ cups water, plus more as needed
2 tablespoons lime juice

PUT THE PEANUT butter, hoisin sauce, and sriracha sauce in a medium saucepan and stir to combine. Whisk in the water until smooth. Heat over medium heat, whisking frequently, just until bubbly and hot, about 5 minutes. The sauce will thicken as it gets hot. Whisk in the lime juice and additional water if the sauce gets too thick. Add more sriracha sauce to taste if you are a spice lover.

Variation: Use lite or full-fat coconut milk in place of part or all of the water for an even richer and creamier sauce.

Per 2 tablespoons: 122 calories, 4 g protein, 8 g fat (1 g sat), 8 g carbohydrates, 185 mg sodium, 10 mg calcium, 1 g fiber

TWENTY YEARS AGO hummus was not so common. Today hummus is available at Subway. Who would have thought this ancient blend of chickpeas and tahini would reach such mainstream heights? Even though it's readily available now, I implore you to give this recipe a whirl. It's a tried-and-true classic that we've enjoyed for decades. Grab a jar of tahini and get going!

Hummus among Us

PUT ALL THE INGREDIENTS in a food processor and process until silky smooth. The longer you process it, the better. Ten minutes isn't too long!

Per $\frac{1}{4}$ cup: 95 calories, 5 g protein, 4 g fat (1 g sat), 10 g carbohydrates, 167 mg sodium, 32 mg calcium, 3 g fiber

MAKES 2 CUPS

1 can (15 ounces) no-salt-added
　chickpeas, rinsed and drained
$\frac{1}{4}$ cup tahini
3 tablespoons lemon juice
1 large clove garlic
$\frac{1}{2}$ teaspoon salt

I BECAME VEGAN for ethical reasons, not because I disliked the taste of meat. So when I first discovered that I could make my own seitan as a hearty meat replacement, right in the comfort of my own home, and that it would be delicious, I never looked back. This recipe makes a large amount, so be prepared. If you want to be traditional, serve this roast with potatoes and gravy, or slice it thinly for sandwiches.

Praise Seitan Vegan Roast

MAKES 8 SERVINGS (1 LARGE ROAST OR 2 SMALLER ROASTS)

4 cloves garlic
1 can (15 ounces) no-salt-added beans (any kind), rinsed and drained
3 tablespoons olive oil
2 tablespoons reduced-sodium tamari
2 cups no-salt-added vegetable broth
1 teaspoon dried oregano
1 teaspoon smoked paprika
1 teaspoon dried thyme
1 teaspoon ground sage
1 teaspoon salt
½ teaspoon freshly ground black pepper
2½ cups vital wheat gluten (see page 11)
½ cup nutritional yeast flakes

PREHEAT THE OVEN to 350 degrees F.

Put the garlic in a food processor and pulse until finely chopped, stopping to scrape down the work bowl with a silicone spatula as needed. Add the beans, oil, and tamari and pulse until almost smooth. Transfer to a large bowl.

Add the broth, oregano, paprika, thyme, sage, salt, and pepper to the bean mixture. Stir with a silicone spatula to combine. Add the vital wheat gluten and nutritional yeast and stir with the spatula until well combined and a dough forms, about 1 minute.

Tear off a piece of foil large enough to accommodate the dough, with enough extra to twist the ends. If you don't have a wide roll of foil, you'll need to use two pieces of foil to make it wide enough. To do this, lay one piece of foil on the counter, then place the second piece on top of it about halfway down. Put the gluten on the foil and shape it into a 10 x 4-inch loaf. Alternatively, make two smaller loaves, each about 5 x 2 inches. Carefully roll the foil over the gluten and twist the ends to seal. Do not roll the foil too tightly because the gluten will expand as it cooks. If you have any concerns about the foil coming undone as the gluten bakes, just roll another piece of foil around the gluten before putting it in the oven.

Transfer to a baking sheet and bake for 45 minutes. Turn the roast over and bake for 45 minutes longer. Let cool completely before slicing.

Tip: This recipe is easily halved, but I prefer to make two smaller roasts and freeze one.

Per serving: 273 calories, 36 g protein, 6 g fat (1 g sat), 17 g carbohydrates, 477 mg sodium, 90 mg calcium, 5 g fiber

YOU KNOW THE QUOTE about laws and sausages, right? The one that says you don't want to see how either of them are made? Well, there's nothing scary about these sausages. Put them on a bun and top them with your favorite condiments, grill them for a cookout, or brown them in a skillet and serve them with pasta. These cruelty-free sausages are both versatile and delicious.

Praise Seitan Lentil-Apple Sausages

PUT THE GARLIC IN a food processor and pulse until finely chopped, stopping to scrape down the work bowl with a silicone spatula as needed. Add the lentils, oil, and tamari and pulse until almost smooth. Transfer to a large bowl.

Add the broth, apple, sage, ginger, thyme, liquid smoke, and pepper to the lentil mixture. Stir with a silicone spatula to combine. Add the vital wheat gluten and nutritional yeast and stir with the spatula until well combined and a dough forms, about 1 minute.

Fit a large saucepan with a steamer basket. Add about 3 inches of water to the saucepan (the water should come just below the steamer basket). Cut eight squares (8 inches each) of foil. Divide the dough into eighths and form each portion into a sausage, about 6 inches in length. Roll the foil around each sausage and twist the ends. Don't roll too tightly as the sausages will expand as they cook. Arrange all the sausages in the steamer basket. Bring the water to a boil over high heat, decrease the heat to medium, cover, and steam for 45 minutes. Let cool completely before slicing or serving.

Per sausage: 284 calories, 36 g protein, 6 g fat (1 g sat), 20 g carbohydrates, 188 mg sodium, 68 mg calcium, 6 g fiber

MAKES 8 SAUSAGES

4 cloves garlic
1 can (15 ounces) no-salt-added green lentils, rinsed and drained
3 tablespoons olive oil
2 tablespoons reduced-sodium tamari
2 cups no-salt-added vegetable broth
1 cup finely minced apple (peeling optional)
1 tablespoon rubbed sage
2 teaspoons ground ginger
1 teaspoon dried thyme
1 teaspoon liquid smoke
$\frac{1}{2}$ teaspoon freshly ground black pepper
$2\frac{1}{2}$ cups vital wheat gluten (see page 11)
$\frac{1}{2}$ cup nutritional yeast flakes

NO TIME TO MARINATE? No problem! This simple go-to recipe will have you covered.

Unmarinated Go-To Tofu or Tempeh

MAKES 4 SERVINGS

1 pound firm or extra-firm
   regular tofu or tempeh, cut
   into ¼-inch-thick slices, cubes,
   or triangles
2 tablespoons reduced-sodium
   tamari
2 tablespoons nutritional
   yeast flakes

MIST A LARGE SKILLET (cast iron if you have one) with cooking spray or coat it with vegetable oil (about 1 teaspoon) and heat over medium-high heat. When the skillet is hot, put in the tofu, arranging it in a single layer with plenty of room; it should sizzle when it touches the skillet. If the skillet isn't large enough to cook all of the tofu without crowding, cook it in batches, adding more cooking spray or oil to the skillet between each batch as needed. Let cook undisturbed until brown and crispy on the bottom, about 5 minutes. Turn the pieces over and let cook undisturbed until brown and crispy on the other side, about 5 minutes. Remove from the heat.

Sprinkle the tamari over the tofu and shake the pan to distribute it evenly. Turn the tofu if necessary so both sides are coated. Sprinkle 1 tablespoon of the nutritional yeast over the tofu and shake the pan to distribute it evenly. Turn the tofu over and sprinkle with the remaining tablespoon of nutritional yeast. Your tofu is ready!

Per serving (with tofu): 191 calories, 20 g protein, 11 g fat (2 g sat), 4 g carbohydrates, 375 mg sodium, 143 mg calcium, 1 g fiber

Per serving (with tempeh): 245 calories, 24 g protein, 13 g fat (4 g sat), 12 g carbohydrates, 371 mg sodium, 121 mg calcium, 1 g fiber

I CAN'T REMEMBER where we first heard about coconut bacon, but whoever thought this up is a straight-up genius. I promise that the first time you taste the smoky, crispy goodness of these flakes you'll have to pick your jaw up from the floor. Try them in a sandwich, sprinkled on a salad, or layered on toast with avocado or peanut butter.

Better-than-Bacon Coconut Flakes

PREHEAT THE OVEN to 300 degrees F. Line a rimmed baking sheet with parchment paper.

Put the coconut flakes in a large bowl. Add the marinade and toss until the flakes are evenly coated. Spread the flakes in a single layer on the lined baking sheet. Bake for 10 minutes. Remove from the oven and flip the flakes over so they cook evenly. Return to the oven and bake until golden brown, about 5 minutes longer. Set the timer! The flakes can go from brown to black in a flash, so watch them closely. Let cool before using (they'll crisp as they cool) and use immediately.

Tip: Better-than-Bacon Coconut Flakes won't stay crispy for more than a few hours, but they'll still be delicious the following day.

Per 2 tablespoons: 97 calories, 0 g protein, 1 g fat (0.1 g sat), 6 g carbohydrates, 61 mg sodium, 8 mg calcium, 0 g fiber

MAKES 1½ CUPS

1½ cups unsweetened large dried coconut flakes (not the tiny bits but big flakes!)
3 tablespoons Better-than-Bacon Marinade (page 77)

THE SECRET TO delicious tofu is revealed! This is a riff on a recipe from the renowned cookbook author Bryanna Clark Grogan, but I've adapted it to reflect our very own Herbivore tofu style. The marinade can be used for a couple of pounds of tofu, so don't toss it after your first batch.

Marinated Go-To Tofu or Tempeh

MAKES 4 SERVINGS

Go-To Marinade (makes 1 cup)

½ cup water
¼ cup nutritional yeast
¼ cup reduced-sodium tamari
1 teaspoon poultry seasoning
¼ teaspoon freshly ground
   black pepper

Go-To Tofu or Tempeh

1 pound firm or extra-firm
   regular tofu or tempeh, cut
   into ¼-inch-thick slices, cubes,
   or triangles
2 tablespoons nutritional
   yeast flakes

PUT ALL THE MARINADE ingredients in a large container with a tight-fitting lid and shake until well combined. Put the tofu in the marinade, cover, and refrigerate for at least 1 hour or up to 4 days.

To cook, mist a large skillet (cast iron if you have one) with cooking spray or coat it with vegetable oil (about 1 teaspoon) and heat over medium-high heat. When the skillet is hot, put in the tofu (leave the marinade behind), arranging it in a single layer with plenty of room; it should sizzle when it touches the skillet. If the skillet isn't large enough to cook all of the tofu without crowding, cook it in batches, adding more cooking spray or oil to the skillet between each batch as needed. Let cook undisturbed until brown and crispy on the bottom, about 5 minutes. Turn the pieces over and let cook undisturbed until brown and crispy on the other side, about 5 minutes. Remove from the heat.

Sprinkle 1 tablespoon of the nutritional yeast over the tofu and shake the pan to distribute it evenly. Turn the tofu over and sprinkle with the remaining tablespoon of nutritional yeast. Your tofu is ready!

Variation: Add 2 teaspoons of hot sauce or 2 teaspoons of liquid smoke to the marinade before adding the tofu.

Per serving (with tofu): 211 calories, 23 g protein, 11 g fat (2 g sat), 6 g carbohydrates, 553 mg sodium, 151 mg calcium, 1 g fiber

Per serving (with tempeh): 265 calories, 26 g protein, 13 g fat (4 g sat), 14 g carbohydrates, 549 mg sodium, 129 mg calcium, 1 g fiber

WE LOVE TO EAT grilled barbecued tofu or tempeh in the summertime. There really is nothing like it, especially when it's grilled with corn and other vegetables. It's totally worth it to make sure the tofu has time to marinate and then give it special treatment on the grill. Use whichever barbecue sauce you love the most or make your own (page 55).

Barbecued Tofu or Tempeh

MIST THE GRATES of a grill or a grill pan with cooking spray. Heat the grill to medium or put the grill pan over medium heat. When hot, arrange the tofu on the grill and cook each side until lightly marked, about 5 minutes.

Pour the barbecue sauce into a shallow bowl. Remove each piece of tofu one at a time and dip it into the sauce until well coated. Return the tofu to the grill. Grill each side again, basting with the sauce, about 3 minutes per side. Flip the pieces around to get nice grill marks, if that's your thing. Regardless of how the tofu looks, it will taste fabulous!

Per serving (with tofu): 253 calories, 15 g protein, 8 g fat (1 g sat), 32 g carbohydrates, 660 mg sodium, 267 mg calcium, 3 g fiber

Per serving (with tempeh): 331 calories, 23 g protein, 8 g fat (2 g sat), 41 g carbohydrates, 662 mg sodium, 141 mg calcium, 7 g fiber

MAKES 4 SERVINGS

1 pound super-firm tofu or tempeh, cut into ½-inch slices and marinated in Go-To Marinade (page 70)

2 cups barbecue sauce

WE OFTEN LIKE our tofu a bit spicy when we add it to one of our bowl recipes, such as Fubonn Bowls (page 150). Here's how we do it.

Spicy Hot Tofu

MAKES 4 SERVINGS

1 package (1 pound) extra-firm or super-firm tofu (marinated or plain), cut into ¼-inch-thick slices, cubes, or triangles

2 tablespoons hot sauce

1 tablespoon reduced-sodium tamari

MIST A LARGE SKILLET (cast iron if you have one) with cooking spray or coat it with vegetable oil (about 1 teaspoon) and heat over medium-high heat. When the skillet is hot, put in the tofu, arranging it in a single layer with plenty of room; it should sizzle when it touches the skillet. If the skillet isn't large enough to cook all of the tofu without crowding, cook it in batches, adding more cooking spray or oil to the skillet between each batch as needed. Let cook undisturbed until brown and crispy on the bottom, about 5 minutes. Turn the pieces over and let cook undisturbed until brown and crispy on the other side, about 5 minutes. Remove from the heat.

Sprinkle the hot sauce and tamari over the tofu and shake the pan to distribute evenly. Turn the tofu if necessary so both sides are coated. Your tofu is ready!

Per serving: 178 calories, 18 g protein, 11 g fat (2 g sat), 3 g carbohydrates, 384 mg sodium, 140 mg calcium, 0 g fiber

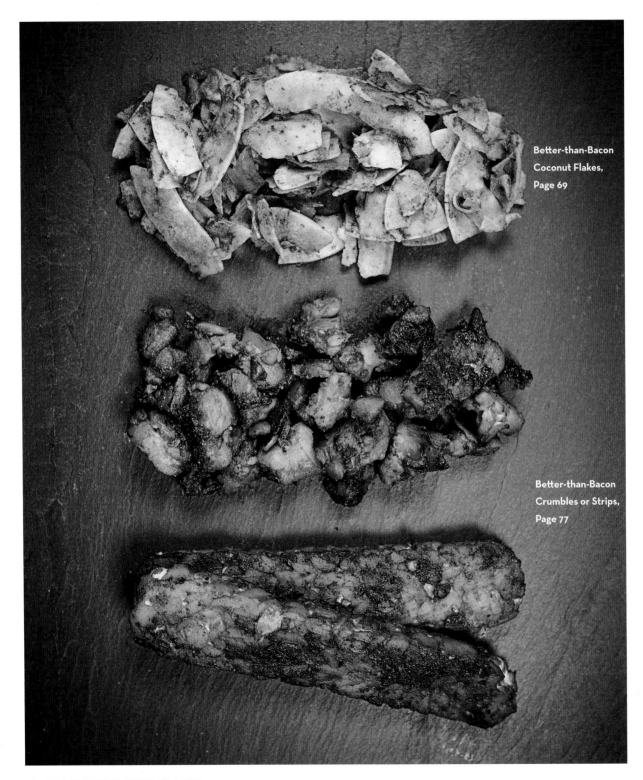

Better-than-Bacon
Coconut Flakes,
Page 69

Better-than-Bacon
Crumbles or Strips,
Page 77

TEMPEH IS A NUTRIENT-RICH, whole-food alternative to meat. We eat these strips with breakfast, use them in BLT sammies, and add them to any dish that could benefit from a hit of bacony flavor. The crumbles are great sprinkled over salads or soups or added to pasta or mac and cheese. Use your imagination!

Better-than-Bacon Crumbles or Strips

TO MAKE THE MARINADE, put all the ingredients in a medium bowl and whisk until well combined.

For crumbles, crumble the tempeh directly into the bowl of marinade. Cover and let marinate in the refrigerator for at least 30 minutes or up to 12 hours.

For strips, cut the tempeh into ¼-inch-thick slices and arrange in a single layer in an 8-inch square glass baking pan. Pour the marinade over the tempeh, cover, and let marinate in the refrigerator for at least 30 minutes or up to 12 hours.

To cook, heat the oil in a large skillet (cast iron if you have one) over medium-high heat. Tilt the skillet so the oil covers the surface evenly. When a drop of water sizzles in the skillet, you'll know the skillet is hot enough and ready. Add the tempeh and any remaining marinade and spread the tempeh out so it's in a single layer. Then, just leave it alone! Let it cook until crispy, 3 to 5 minutes. Flip the tempeh over or shuffle the crumbles around using a thin metal spatula. Continue cooking until the tempeh is as crispy as you like, about 10 minutes longer. Serve immediately or let cool in the pan until ready to use.

Per serving: 343 calories, 26 g protein, 19 g fat (4 g sat), 19 g carbohydrates, 623 mg sodium, 166 mg calcium, 8 g fiber

MAKES 2 SERVINGS

Better-than-Bacon Marinade (makes ½ cup)
3 tablespoons reduced-sodium tamari
1 tablespoon olive oil
1 tablespoon ketchup
1 tablespoon maple syrup
1 tablespoon liquid smoke
1 teaspoon garlic granules

Tempeh
1 package (8 ounces) tempeh
1 tablespoon olive oil

THIS RECIPE WAS created especially for people like us who don't live in areas where good fresh tomatoes are available year-round. It will get you through the cold months when a decent tomato is impossible to find.

Slow-Roasted Tomatoes

PREHEAT THE OVEN to 250 degrees F. Line a baking sheet with parchment paper.

Put the oil, vinegar, sugar, and salt in a large bowl and whisk until well combined. Add the tomatoes and stir gently to coat. Arrange the tomatoes on the lined baking sheet, cut-side up. Bake until shriveled and the edges begin to brown, 1 to 2 hours.

Tip: The baking time will depend on the size of the tomatoes. Just take one out and taste it. You'll know it's done when it's a bit chewy and the super-sweet taste knocks you on the floor.

Per serving: 59 calories, 1 g protein, 5 g fat (1 g sat), 4 g carbohydrates, 40 mg sodium, 56 mg calcium, 1 g fiber

MAKES 4 SERVINGS

1 tablespoon olive oil
1 tablespoon balsamic vinegar
1 teaspoon sugar or agave nectar
Pinch salt
1 package (1 pound) cherry
    tomatoes, halved

PIZZA DOUGH IS VERY easy to make and comes with a real sense of accomplishment. Although you can find decent pizza dough at a store, it just feels good knowing you made your pizza from top to bottom.

Mostly Whole Wheat Pizza Dough

MAKES ENOUGH FOR TWO 12-INCH ROUNDS OR 1 RECTANGULAR JELLY-ROLL PAN

1¼ cups warm water
2¼ teaspoons (1 packet) active dry yeast
1 teaspoon sugar
2 cups white whole wheat flour
1 cup unbleached all-purpose flour
1 teaspoon salt
1 tablespoon olive oil

PUT THE WATER, yeast, and sugar in a measuring cup, stir to combine, and set aside for 5 minutes. It should get foamy. If it doesn't foam, the yeast has expired, and you'll have to start over with fresh yeast.

Put the whole wheat flour, all-purpose flour, and salt in a large bowl. Stir with a whisk to combine.

Stir the oil into the yeast mixture, then pour the yeast mixture into the flour. Mix with a large wooden spoon until all the flour is incorporated and a dough forms. Knead in the bowl for 1 to 2 minutes, forming a large ball.

Mist a separate large bowl with cooking spray and put the dough in it. Cover with a clean kitchen towel and let rest until doubled, about 1 hour. Punch down the dough and knead in the bowl for 30 seconds. Now, roll it out and make pizza!

Tip: This dough is best when used the same day it's made, but it will keep in the fridge for a couple of days if it's well wrapped in plastic or stored in an airtight container. Just be sure to let it come to room temperature before you try to roll it out.

Cornmeal Pizza Crust: Replace ½ cup of the all-purpose flour with ½ cup of yellow cornmeal.

Per serving (based on 8 servings): 184 calories, 6 g protein, 2 g fat (0.3 g sat), 35 g carbohydrates, 296 mg sodium, 11 mg calcium, 4 g fiber

IT'S AN UNWRITTEN RULE THAT we Herbivores have a salad at least once a day. My belief is that a meal isn't a meal if it doesn't have something green on the plate. These salads are your on-ramp to the vegan superhighway, with familiar stops and some new sights to see. Kale, for example, has become such a popular leafy green in salads for good reason, and we love it. It will never go out of style at our house.

Soup, however, is a more complicated story. When we first met, Josh told me, "Soup is futile." He considered soup "salty water in a can," because that's what he grew up eating. And for years he claimed that he detested soup. But now that he's tried my homemade versions, his tune has thankfully changed. While he isn't chanting for tomato soup the way our daughter, Ruby, does, he now freely admits (as he devours bowl after bowl of it) that soup can be satisfying and deserves respect.

Salads & Soups

Smoky Cauliflower Soup with Fennel,
Carrot, and Potato, Page 98

I DON'T LIKE TO waste superlatives. When people say that something changed their lives, I roll my eyes along with everyone else and chalk it up to a familial tendency toward exaggeration. But I'm not kidding or overstating the truth when I say just how much this simple salad has had an impact on my life. It gets my family eating lots of raw leafy greens. It gets my grade-schooler exclaiming loudly and excitedly, "Kale salad, kale salad, kale salad, kale salad!" Mother of the year? That's me.

Only-Kale-Can-Save-Us-Now Salad

TO MAKE THE DRESSING, put the tahini, lemon juice, tamari, nutritional yeast, flax meal, onion granules, and garlic granules in a large bowl (large enough to accommodate the kale leaves). Add the water and whisk to combine, adding more water if the dressing seems too thick. (Tahini varies in consistency.)

Add the kale leaves to the dressing and mix using your hands. Don't be shy now! Rub the dressing into the kale and make sure to distribute it evenly. Sprinkle the optional hemp seeds over the top if desired. Serve immediately or store in a covered container in the fridge for up to 2 days.

Tip: Before you get started, you'll need to clean and prepare the kale. Hold the stem of a kale leaf in one hand, and with your other hand pull the leaf up the stem. When you've removed all the leaves from the stems, tear the leaves into bite-sized pieces (you can compost the stems). Give the leaves a good bath in cold water, and spin them dry in a salad spinner.

Per serving: 142 calories, 8 g protein, 5 g fat (1 g sat), 22 g carbohydrates, 437 mg sodium, 218 mg calcium, 3 g fiber

MAKES 4 SERVINGS

2 tablespoons tahini
2 tablespoons lemon juice
2 tablespoons reduced-sodium tamari
2 tablespoons nutritional yeast flakes
1 tablespoon flax meal
2 teaspoons onion granules
1 teaspoon garlic granules
¼ cup water, plus more as needed
9 cups torn curly kale leaves (about 1 bunch), in bite-sized pieces (see tip)
⅓ cup hemp seeds or chopped raw sunflower seeds (optional)

IT DRIVES ME BONKERS to see salad recipes that are full of meat, dairy, and eggs. I know people have a hard time getting enough vegetables in their mouths, but it certainly isn't helping the cause when a few paltry lettuce leaves are drowning in animal products. What good is that? Who the heck knows. What I do know is this salad is all plants and all amazing. Chop, chop, chop your way to crunchy salad heaven, and top it off with spicy chickpeas and Creamy Tarragon Ranch Dressing. Now we're talkin' salad!

Chopped Salad with Spicy Hot Chickpeas

MAKES 4 LARGE SERVINGS

Chopped Salad

4 cups stemmed and chopped curly kale leaves (see tip, page 83)

2 hearts romaine lettuce, chopped

2 cups chopped asparagus, blanched and drained (see tip)

1 cup chopped roasted red peppers (jarred is fine)

1 cup fresh or thawed frozen corn kernels

1 cup chopped cucumber

1 cup chopped tomato

1 cup diced avocado

½ cup chopped dill pickles

⅓ cup unsalted roasted sunflower seeds (see tip)

½ cup Creamy Tarragon Ranch Dressing (page 43), plus more as desired

Spicy Hot Chickpeas

1 teaspoon olive oil (optional)

1 can (15 ounces) no-salt-added chickpeas, rinsed and drained

2 tablespoons hot sauce

1 teaspoon reduced-sodium tamari

TO MAKE THE SALAD, layer the kale, lettuce, asparagus, red peppers, corn, cucumber, tomato, avocado, and pickles in a large bowl and chill in the refrigerator.

To make the chickpeas, put the oil in a large skillet (cast iron if you have one) or mist with cooking spray and heat over medium heat. When the skillet is hot, add the chickpeas and shake the pan briefly to evenly distribute the oil over them. Let cook, shaking the pan occasionally so the chickpeas cook evenly, until browned all over, 12 to 15 minutes. While the chickpeas cook, put the hot sauce and tamari in a small bowl and stir to combine. When the chickpeas are brown and crisp, pour the hot-sauce mixture in the center of the skillet and shake the pan or stir well to combine. Add the hot chickpeas to the chilled salad, dress with the Creamy Tarragon Ranch Dressing, toss until evenly distributed, and serve.

Tips: To blanch the asparagus, put the chopped pieces in a small saucepan and barely cover with water. Bring to a boil, then remove from the heat. Let the asparagus sit in the water for 1 minute, then drain, rinse with cold water to stop the cooking, and drain again. If time permits, chill the blanched asparagus in the refrigerator before assembling the salad.

To toast the sunflower seeds, heat them in a small skillet over high heat, shaking the skillet frequently, until fragrant, 3 to 5 minutes. Let cool on a plate before adding to the salad.

Per serving: 454 calories, 16 g protein, 12 g fat (3 g sat), 53 g carbohydrates, 904 mg sodium, 312 mg calcium, 14 g fiber

WE ALWAYS SERVE THIS at our Thanksgiving feast. It's important to have lots of green at the table to balance out all the deliciously beige holiday food (I'm looking at you, potatoes and gravy). This slaw is crunchy, savory, and sweet, and the very thinly sliced Brussels sprouts help mask the fact that they actually are, well, raw Brussels sprouts. I make this early in the day so the flavors have time to mingle.

Brussels Sprouts Slaw with Walnuts, Apricots, and Garlic Aïoli

PUT THE BRUSSELS SPROUTS, mayonnaise, walnuts, apricots, garlic, and lemon juice in a large bowl and toss until evenly combined. Season with salt and pepper to taste and toss again.

Tip: To toast the walnuts, heat a small skillet over medium-high heat. When hot, add the walnuts and toast, stirring frequently, until they turn a shade or two darker and are fragrant, 3 to 5 minutes. To keep the walnuts from burning, remove from the heat immediately and transfer to a plate to cool. If you prepare the salad in advance, add the walnuts just before serving.

Per serving: 201 calories, 3 g protein, 15 g fat (1g sat), 12 g carbohydrates, 132 mg sodium, 35 mg calcium, 4 g fiber

Note: Analysis doesn't include salt to taste.

MAKES 6 SERVINGS

1 pound Brussels sprouts, trimmed and very finely sliced (use a mandoline or a sharp knife)
½ cup vegan mayonnaise
¼ cup chopped walnuts, toasted (see tip)
¼ cup thinly sliced dried apricots
1 teaspoon minced or pressed garlic
½ teaspoon lemon juice
Salt
Freshly ground black pepper

HERE'S A DISH THAT TAKES me back to our early vegan days. We loved faux feta so much and used it on salads several times a week. Spinach was the fancy green in our diets back then; kale wasn't even on our radar. Now we know to add more color and texture to a salad, and this one really delivers. Salty olives, crunchy seeds, sweet oranges, and just the right dressing. This salad is grocery-store exotic!

Spinach Salad with Feta, Tomato, Olives, and Cucumber

MAKES 4 SERVINGS

1 bag (5 ounces) baby spinach

1 cup segmented, seeded, and chopped orange

1 cup sliced cucumber, in half-moons

½ cup diced tomato

⅓ cup sliced kalamata olives

1 cup So Faux Feta (page 47) plus 2 tablespoons marinade

¼ cup raw pumpkin seeds, toasted (see tip)

LAYER THE SPINACH, orange, cucumber, tomato, and olives in a large salad bowl. Sprinkle the feta and marinade over the salad. Top with the pumpkin seeds. Toss just before serving.

Tip: To toast the pumpkin seeds, heat a small skillet over medium-high heat. When hot, add the pumpkin seeds and toast, stirring frequently, until they turn a shade or two darker and are fragrant, 3 to 4 minutes. To keep the seeds from burning, remove from the heat immediately and transfer to a plate to cool. If you prepare the salad in advance, add the seeds just before serving.

Per serving: 196 calories, 9 g protein, 11 g fat (2 g sat), 13 g carbohydrates, 450 mg sodium, 144 mg calcium, 3 g fiber

VEGANS GET ACCUSED of eating a lot of salads, as if that's a bad thing. Yet there are plenty of vegans who don't eat salad any more often than their meat-eating accusers. Instead of the shriveled-iceberg-lettuce-wedge-with-a-tomato-slice disaster many people grew up with, heed the call of dark leafy greens. And when you want something to really fill your belly, add smoky, crispy tempeh and savory sun-dried tomatoes. Boom. Salad for dinner.

Kale, Tempeh, and Tomato Salad

MAKES 4 SERVINGS

9 cups torn curly kale leaves
   (about 1 bunch), in bite-sized
   pieces (see tip, page 83)
1 teaspoon lemon juice
1 teaspoon olive oil
¼ teaspoon salt
⅓ cup vegan mayonnaise
⅓ cup finely chopped sun-
   dried tomatoes (preferably
   not packed in oil), or 1 cup
   Slow-Roasted Tomatoes
   (page 79)
2 teaspoons garlic granules
1 recipe Better-than-Bacon
   Crumbles or Strips (page 77)

PUT THE KALE IN a large bowl. Pour the lemon juice and oil over the kale and sprinkle with the salt. Massage the kale leaves with your hands, distributing the liquid and salt evenly over all the leaves, until the kale turns a shade darker and has wilted a bit, 2 to 3 minutes. Carefully drain any liquid from the bottom of the bowl, as it will be bitter. Add the mayonnaise, tomatoes, and garlic granules and work the dressing in using your hands. Just before serving, add the crumbles and toss until evenly distributed.

Per serving: 386 calories, 16 g protein, 33 g fat (4 g sat), 26 g carbohydrates, 717 mg sodium, 269 mg calcium, 3 g fiber

SO OFTEN PEOPLE MISS out on the magic of salads. Think of that empty bowl as a blank canvas. Need a lot of protein? Pile on the beans and whole grains. Got a great deal on baby lettuce or spinach? Keep your salad simple to enjoy the freshness of the greens. Carbo-loading for a long hike or bike ride? Add rice to your creation. Need something substantial to hold you all day? Include a hearty green, avocado, and tofu or tempeh, and toss with a creamy dressing. Salad can be a side dish or a giant, filling meal. Just stare into that empty bowl and envision what you want.

Here are more than fifty ingredients you can put in a salad. What can you add to this list?

More than Fifty Ingredients to Put in a Salad

apples
apricots, dried
arugula
avocado
bean sprouts, fresh
beans (any kind), cooked
beet, roasted or raw shredded
bell pepper
broccoli, raw or steamed
carrot, grated
cashews, raw or toasted
celery
chard, baby
chiles, mild or hot
corn kernels, raw or cooked
cranberries, dried
croutons
cucumber
granola

grapes
hemp seeds
herbs (basil, cilantro, dill, parsley), fresh
hummus
kale, baby
lentils, cooked
mesclun
mint, fresh
nutritional yeast flakes
olives
orange segments
peanuts
pepperoncini
pickles
pumpkin seeds, raw or toasted
quinoa, cooked
raisins
red onion

rice (any kind), cooked
romaine
root vegetables, roasted
salsa
scallions
spinach, baby
sunflower seeds, raw or toasted
tempeh
tofu
tomatoes, fresh
tomatoes, sun-dried
vegan bacon bits
vegan cheese
vegan chicken strips
vegan Parmesan
vegan sour cream
vegetables, grilled
vegetables, pickled
walnuts

WHEN YOU'RE NOT UP FOR chomping on a whole piece of fruit and would rather sit down with a fork, whip this up. Everyone will think you're super fancy! Choose fruits you love that are in season, such as apples, bananas, blueberries, cherries, grapes, kiwis, mangoes, nectarines, oranges, papayas, peaches, pears, pineapples, raspberries, or strawberries. A combination of at least three makes for a great fruit salad.

Maple-Mint Fruit Salad

MAKES 4 CUPS

4 cups chopped fresh
   fruit or berries
¼ cup chopped fresh mint,
   lightly packed
2 tablespoons maple syrup
1 tablespoon lemon juice

PUT THE FRUIT IN A large bowl. Add the mint, maple syrup, and lemon juice and toss gently to combine. Serve immediately.

Per cup: 91 calories, 0 g protein, 0 g fat (0 g sat), 20 g carbohydrates, 3 mg sodium, 28 mg calcium, 4 g fiber

PEOPLE OFTEN PUT DOWN vegans by saying we're just a bunch of crunchy hippies who eat nothing but salad and granola. Clearly these stereotypes are outdated, because all kinds of people have chosen this cruelty-free lifestyle. Now, friends, with that said, can I reasonably expect to present a salad with granola on top and still claim to be fighting this stereotype? You bet I can, because this salad rules, and I wouldn't know a Grateful Dead song if it ran over me in a Volkswagen van. Okay, full disclosure. We own a Volkswagen van, but we mostly listen to heavy metal in it.

Crunchy Hippie Granola Salad

PUT THE BABY GREENS, romaine hearts, cucumber, apple, and apricots in a large salad bowl. Add the dressing and toss until evenly distributed. Just before serving, sprinkle the granola over the top of the salad or put the granola in a cute bowl with a spoon and pass it at the table.

Variation: Replace the apricots with any other dried fruit of your choice.

Per serving: 204 calories, 4 g protein, 14 g fat (1 g sat), 16 g carbohydrates, 366 mg sodium, 30 mg calcium, 3 g fiber

MAKES 6 SERVINGS

2 cups mixed baby greens
2 romaine hearts, chopped into 2-inch pieces
1 cup diced cucumber
1 cup diced apple or pear
¼ cup dried apricots, thinly sliced
½ cup Herbivore House Dressing (page 42)
1 cup granola or Northwest Granola (page 20)

THIS SOUP IS THE first recipe I ever created, and it's still my favorite split pea soup. It's the first soup I make every fall, at the beginning of the Portland rainy season. You can use green split peas if you prefer; the soup just won't be sunshine yellow.

Sunny Split Pea Soup

PUT THE OIL IN a large soup pot over medium heat. When hot, add the onion and garlic and cook, stirring frequently, until the onion just starts to brown, about 5 minutes. Add the carrot, broccoli stalk, and bell pepper and cook, stirring frequently, for 5 minutes. Stir in the bay leaf, sage, thyme, and rosemary. Cook, stirring frequently, for 1 minute. Add the broth, water, and split peas. Increase the heat to medium-high and bring to a boil. Decrease the heat to low, cover, and simmer, stirring occasionally, until the peas begin to break down and thicken the soup, 45 to 60 minutes. Add the chard, stir, and cook until the chard is wilted and tender, about 10 minutes. Stir in the parsley and lemon juice. Season with salt and pepper to taste.

Per cup: 132 calories, 9 g protein, 2 g fat (0.3 g sat), 29 g carbohydrates, 88 mg sodium, 50 mg calcium, 11 g fiber

Note: Analysis doesn't include salt to taste.

MAKES 8 CUPS

1 tablespoon olive oil
1 cup chopped onion
3 cloves garlic, minced
1 cup chopped carrot
1 cup chopped peeled broccoli stalk or celery
1 yellow, red, or orange bell pepper, diced
1 bay leaf
1 teaspoon rubbed sage
1 teaspoon dried thyme
½ teaspoon dried rosemary
3 cups no-salt-added vegetable broth
2 cups water
1½ cups yellow split peas, soaked in 2 cups of water for 1 hour and drained
4 cups stemmed and chopped Swiss chard
¼ cup chopped fresh parsley
¼ cup lemon juice
Salt
Freshly ground pepper

WHEN JOSH AND I were children, our tomato soup came from a can. Josh thought that was all tomato soup had to offer. He was as wrong as wrong could be. We are proud to say that Ruby, our daughter, loves tomato soup, but it's our creamy, tangy, homemade version, full of nourishment and flavor.

Ruby's Tomato Soup

MAKES 4 CUPS

1 tablespoon olive oil
1½ cups finely chopped onions
2 large cloves garlic, minced
2 tablespoons no-salt-added tomato paste
1 teaspoon agave nectar
1 teaspoon dried thyme
½ teaspoon dried basil
1 can (15 ounces) no-salt-added diced tomatoes, with juice
2 cups no-salt-added vegetable broth
2 tablespoons nutritional yeast flakes
1 cup plain soy creamer, unsweetened soy milk, or additional vegetable broth
2 teaspoons balsamic vinegar

HEAT THE OIL IN A medium soup pot over medium heat. When hot, add the onions and garlic and cook, stirring frequently, until the onions just start to brown, about 5 minutes. Add the tomato paste, agave nectar, thyme, and basil and mix well to create a paste. Cook, stirring once or twice, for 3 minutes. Add the tomatoes and their juice, 1 cup of the broth, and the nutritional yeast and stir to combine. Process until smooth using an immersion blender. Alternatively, transfer to a blender, process in batches until smooth, and return to the pot. Stir in the remaining cup of broth and the soy creamer and heat over medium heat, stirring frequently, until hot, about 15 minutes. Stir in the vinegar just before serving.

Per cup: 171 calories, 4 g protein, 3 g fat (1 g sat), 21 g carbohydrates, 40 mg sodium, 54 mg calcium, 4 g fiber

SALADS & SOUPS **97**

SMOKED PAPRIKA IS A magical spice. It transforms this humble vegetable soup into a delicious star attraction while imparting a gorgeous color. Cashew Cream and sherry vinegar add richness and sophistication. This is a great soup to serve to friends when you want to impress them with your culinary talents.

Smoky Cauliflower Soup with Fennel, Carrot, and Potato

MAKES 8 CUPS

1 tablespoon olive oil
1 cup finely chopped onion
1½ cups chopped fennel bulb
1 cup peeled and diced potato
¾ cup chopped carrot
1 tablespoon minced garlic
3 cups cauliflower florets
   (1 small head)
1 tablespoon chopped fresh
   parsley, or 1 teaspoon dried
2 teaspoons smoked paprika
4 cups no-salt-added
   chicken-style broth or
   vegetable broth
1 cup Cashew Cream (page 56),
   plain soy creamer, or
   unsweetened soy milk
Salt
Freshly ground pepper
2 tablespoons sherry vinegar

HEAT THE OIL IN A large soup pot over medium heat. When hot, add the onion and cook, stirring frequently, until the onion just starts to brown, about 5 minutes. Add the fennel, potato, carrot, and garlic and cook, stirring frequently, for 5 minutes. Add the cauliflower, parsley, and paprika and stir to combine. Decrease the heat to low, cover, and cook, stirring occasionally, for 15 minutes. Add the broth, increase the heat to medium-high, and bring to a boil. Decrease the heat to medium-low, cover, and simmer for 30 minutes. Crush the cauliflower using a potato masher until it's broken into little pieces. Put 2 cups of the soup in a blender and process until smooth. Pour the blended mixture back in the pot and stir in the Cashew Cream. Increase the heat to medium and simmer, stirring occasionally, until heated through, about 5 minutes. Season with salt and pepper to taste. Stir in the vinegar just before serving.

Per cup: 130 calories, 4 g protein, 7 g fat (2 g sat), 14 g carbohydrates, 53 mg sodium, 34 mg calcium, 4 g fiber

Note: Analysis doesn't include salt to taste.

I ADMIT IT. I HAVE a thing for lentil soup. I love it. Any color lentil will do, as will any flavor combo. Bring it on. But this lentil soup is one that even those who don't love lentils will adore. Red lentils cook quickly, making this soup fabulous for nights when you just want to toss everything in a pot and read the news or catch up on the latest Herbivore Instagram.

Coconut Curry Red Lentil Soup

HEAT THE OIL IN A large soup pot over medium heat. When hot, add the onions and garlic and cook, stirring frequently, until the onions just start to brown, about 5 minutes. Add the potatoes, curry powder, and optional cayenne and stir to mix. Stir in the broth and lentils. Increase the heat to high and bring to a boil. Decrease the heat to medium-low, cover, and cook until the potatoes are tender, about 20 minutes. Process until smooth using an immersion blender. Alternatively, transfer to a blender, process in batches until smooth, and return to the pot. Stir in the coconut milk and simmer over medium heat until hot, 5 to 8 minutes. Season with salt to taste. Stir in the lime juice just before serving.

Per cup: 227 calories, 11 g protein, 5 g fat (3 g sat), 35 g carbohydrates, 25 mg sodium, 30 mg calcium, 8 g fiber

Note: Analysis doesn't include salt to taste.

MAKES 8 CUPS

1 tablespoon olive oil or coconut oil
2 cups finely chopped onions
2 tablespoons minced garlic
1½ cups peeled and diced potatoes
1 tablespoon curry powder
Pinch cayenne (optional)
5 cups no-salt-added vegetable broth
1½ cups dried red lentils, soaked in 2 cups water for 1 hour and drained
1 can (14 ounces) reduced-fat coconut milk
Salt
3 tablespoons lime juice

ONE OF OUR GOALS with this book was to help new vegans replace non-vegan foods they might be craving. Chicken noodle soup was in heavy rotation when we were kids, so we thought we should give it a shot. Boy are we glad we did! The first taste of this soup brought back a flood of happy childhood memories. We realized that these flavors are hard-wired into us at this point, so why not embrace them?

No-Bird Noodle Soup

TO PREPARE THE TOFU, put the oil in a large skillet (cast iron if you have one) or mist with cooking spray and heat over medium-high heat. When hot, add the tofu; it should sizzle. Don't crowd the tofu (cook in batches if your skillet isn't large enough to hold the full amount). Let it cook undisturbed until crispy and brown on the bottom, about 5 minutes. Turn the pieces over and let the other side cook undisturbed until crispy and brown, about 5 minutes. Remove from the heat. Sprinkle the tamari over the tofu and shake the skillet to coat all the pieces evenly on both sides. Sprinkle half the nutritional yeast over the tofu and shake the skillet to distribute it evenly. Turn the tofu over and sprinkle with the remaining nutritional yeast.

To prepare the soup, heat the oil in a large soup pot over medium heat. When hot, add the carrots, celery, onion, and garlic. Cook, stirring frequently, until the onion starts to brown, about 5 minutes. Stir in the bay leaf, thyme, parsley, and a few grindings of pepper. Add the broth, increase the heat to high, and bring to a boil. Add the pasta, decrease the heat to medium, and cook, stirring once or twice, for 6 minutes. Stir in the reserved tofu and any nutritional yeast in the skillet. Cover and cook for 10 minutes. Season with salt and additional pepper to taste. Stir in the lemon juice just before serving.

Per serving: 587 calories, 26 g protein, 10 g fat (1.4 g sat), 101 g carbohydrates, 315 mg sodium, 123 mg calcium, 9 g fiber

Note: Analysis doesn't include salt to taste.

MAKES 4 SERVINGS

Tofu Chicken

1 teaspoon olive oil
8 ounces extra-firm or super-firm tofu, cut into $\frac{1}{2}$-inch cubes
1 tablespoon reduced-sodium tamari
1 tablespoon nutritional yeast flakes

Soup

1 teaspoon olive oil
1½ cups finely chopped carrots
1½ cups finely chopped celery
1 cup finely chopped onion
2 cloves garlic, minced
1 bay leaf
1 teaspoon dried thyme
1 teaspoon dried parsley
Freshly ground black pepper
6 cups no-salt-added chicken-style broth
8 ounces angel hair pasta, spaghetti, or fettuccine noodles, broken into bite-sized pieces
Salt
1 tablespoon lemon juice

CHILI IS A POWERHOUSE dish: nutritionally (can't do better than beans), socially (perfect for sports-related parties and potlucks), and functionally (eat it now, eat it tomorrow, or freeze it and eat it in six months). This chili is a breeze to make and has a good range of flavors. We went easy on the heat, but if you want to ramp it up, just add some habanero or jalapeño chiles or mild, smoky chipotles. You can also dial up the cayenne if you like to sweat while you eat.

Herbivore Chili

MAKES 4 SERVINGS

½ cup dried green lentils, rinsed and drained

1½ cups water

2 tablespoons olive oil

2 cups chopped onions

1 cup diced red bell pepper

½ cup diced poblano chile

1 can (4 ounces) mild or hot green chiles, drained

4 large cloves garlic, minced

1 tablespoon chili powder

2 teaspoons ground cumin

1 teaspoon smoked paprika

¼ teaspoon cayenne

1 cup beer or no-salt-added vegetable broth

1 can (28 ounces) no-salt-added crushed tomatoes

1 can (15 ounces) no-salt-added black beans, rinsed and drained

1 can (15 ounces) no-salt-added pinto beans, rinsed and drained

1 cup no-salt-added vegetable broth

1 cup fresh or frozen corn kernels

1 ounce vegan dark chocolate

Salt

2 tablespoons lime juice

PUT THE LENTILS IN a small saucepan. Add the water and bring to a boil over high heat. Decrease the heat to medium, cover, and simmer until the lentils are soft but not mushy, 30 to 35 minutes. Drain and set aside.

Put the olive oil in a large soup pot and heat over medium heat. When hot, add the onions, bell pepper, poblano chile, green chiles, and garlic. Cook, stirring occasionally, until the onions soften, about 10 minutes. Add the chili powder, cumin, paprika, and cayenne and stir to combine. Cook, stirring occasionally, until parts of the vegetables start to stick to the saucepan. Pour in the beer to deglaze the saucepan and stir, scraping up any bits that are stuck on the bottom. Increase the heat to medium-high and simmer for 10 minutes. Add the tomatoes, reserved lentils, black beans, pinto beans, broth, and corn and stir to combine. Bring to a boil. Decrease the heat to medium, cover, and cook, stirring occasionally, for 30 minutes. Stir in the chocolate and cook, stirring occasionally, for 5 minutes. Season with salt to taste. Stir in the lime juice just before serving.

Serving suggestion: Go crazy with toppings! Try diced avocado, shredded cabbage, chopped fresh tomatoes, sliced scallions, sliced jalapeño chiles, shredded vegan cheese, crumbled tortilla chips, or a spoonful of vegan sour cream or yogurt. You get the idea. And why not serve the chili over rice? Or with Spicy Corn Muffins (page 158) on the side? Or ladled over pasta, like they do in Cincinnati?

Per cup: 217 calories, 10 g protein, 5 g fat (1 g sat), 34 g carbohydrates, 61 mg sodium, 83 mg calcium, 11 g fiber

Note: Analysis doesn't include salt to taste.

"WOULD YOU LIKE FRIES WITH THAT?" The sad truth is that deep-fried potatoes are the most commonly eaten vegetable in America. I feel bad for people who don't know about other vegetables or side dishes! It's tragic, really. We keep the preparation of our vegetables dishes simple and often serve more than one with a meal. And while we still love potatoes, ours rarely see the deep-fryer. We recommend that you try different combinations of simply prepared greens with sauces from Basics and Staples (page 41). Then, whip up some Polenta Fries (page 110) and Skillet Chickpeas (page 119), and you'll have a fine meal of sides for yourself.

Sides

Skillet Chickpeas, Page 119

THESE ARE CALLED "everyday" fries because they are baked with very little oil. That means you can enjoy fries every day if you want, without the massive amount of fat you'd be eating if these were deep-fried white potatoes. And sweet potatoes offer a lot of nutrition, more than comes with the standard American French fry. They are also called "everyday" because our daughter, Ruby, wants to eat sweet potatoes every day, and this is one of her favorite ways.

Everyday Sweet Potato Fries

PREHEAT THE OVEN to 450 degrees F. Line a rimmed baking sheet with parchment paper.

Put the sweet potatoes in a large bowl. Sprinkle with the oil, tamari, and pepper and toss until evenly distributed. Arrange in a single layer on the lined baking sheet, making sure that no potatoes touch; they each need a little space to cook. Bake for 15 minutes. Remove from the oven and shake potatoes around a bit so they don't stick. Bake for 10 to 15 minutes longer, until they are cooked through and tender.

Variation: Add one or more of the following along with the olive oil: 2 tablespoons of hot sauce, 2 tablespoons of chili powder, 1 tablespoon of lime juice plus 2 teaspoons of ground cumin, minced fresh garlic or garlic granules (as much as you like), 2 teaspoons of smoked paprika.

Per serving: 174 calories, 3 g protein, 7 g fat (1 g sat), 26 g carbohydrates, 249 mg sodium, 44 mg calcium, 4 g fiber

MAKES 4 SERVINGS

4 medium sweet potatoes, scrubbed and cut lengthwise into eighths
2 tablespoons olive oil
1 tablespoon reduced-sodium tamari
½ teaspoon freshly ground black pepper

IF THE MIGHTY FRENCH fry and the humble baked potato had a child, this recipe would be it. Crushing the potato breaks open the skin and lets the inside of the potato pop out. It then gets crispy like a French fry, but without the deep-frying. These do take some time in the oven, but this is as fuss-free a side dish as it gets.

Crushed and Crispy Potatoes

MAKES 4 SERVINGS

8 medium (plus more if you want leftovers—and you really do, trust me) russet, gold, or red-skinned potatoes, scrubbed and pierced with a knife
2 tablespoons olive oil
Salt
Freshly ground black pepper

PUT A RACK IN the center of the oven. Preheat the oven to 450 degrees F. Line a rimmed baking sheet with parchment paper.

Rub each potato all over with some of the olive oil. Put the potatoes on the lined baking sheet and sprinkle with a bit of salt. Bake for 35 minutes. Turn the potatoes over so they can brown on the other side (the skins should be getting crispy) and bake for 20 minutes longer. Don't turn off the oven.

Flatten each potato using a metal potato masher or metal spatula. Hold the baking sheet steady with one hand (wear an oven mitt!) and crush each potato with the other. Once all the potatoes have been smooshed, brush the remaining oil over them and sprinkle with salt and pepper. Bake for 15 minutes, until the exposed potato flesh is golden brown.

Variation: Sprinkle chili powder or za'atar over the potatoes before or after baking, or sprinkle with Better-than-Bacon Coconut Flakes (page 69) or chopped fresh herbs after baking.

Per serving: 395 calories, 9 g protein, 7 g fat (1 g sat), 74 g carbohydrates, 28 mg sodium, 62 mg calcium, 8 g fiber

Note: Analysis doesn't include salt to taste.

"MASHED ROOTS" SOUNDS like a jam band from our hippie-heavy neighbor to the south, Eugene. But I assure you, this comfort-food delight won't play one song for forty minutes and ask to crash at your house afterward. That's because it can't; it's just root vegetables. But not ordinary root vegetables. This combo is rich and creamy and loaded with flavor. We like to leave the skins on our potatoes, but feel free to peel yours if that's not your thing.

Go-To Mashed Roots

MAKES 4 SERVINGS

6 medium Yukon gold potatoes, scrubbed and quartered
1 medium parsnip, peeled and cut into 1-inch pieces
1 medium rutabaga or turnip, peeled and cut into 1-inch pieces
½ cup unsweetened soy milk or soy creamer
3 tablespoons olive oil
1 teaspoon salt
Freshly ground black pepper
Vegan butter (optional)

PUT THE POTATOES, parsnip, and rutabaga in a large saucepan. Cover with water and bring to a boil over high heat. Decrease the heat to medium-low and simmer until all of the vegetables are soft, 10 to 15 minutes. Drain and return to the saucepan.

While the vegetables are cooking, put the soy milk in a small saucepan and heat over medium heat until steaming, 3 to 4 minutes. Alternatively, heat the soy milk in a microwave.

Pour the hot soy milk and oil over the vegetables. Mash with a potato masher or hand mixer. Add the salt. Season with pepper and vegan butter, if using, to taste and mash some more.

Per serving: 399 calories, 9 g protein, 11 g fat (2 g sat), 70 g carbohydrates, 618 mg sodium, 128 mg calcium, 8 g fiber

POLENTA IS COARSELY ground yellow cornmeal that cooks into a creamy porridge. I'm not sure why polenta isn't as popular as pasta since it's just as simple and delicious. Give this basic recipe a try and soon you'll be making all kinds of wonderful variations.

Go-To Polenta

PUT THE WATER, broth, and salt in a large saucepan and bring to a boil over medium-high heat. Slowly whisk in the cornmeal, stirring constantly. The polenta will thicken quickly and bubble (stand back to avoid splatters). Decrease the heat to low (keep stirring!) and stir in the nutritional yeast. Cover and cook, stirring frequently to prevent sticking, until the polenta is as thick as you like it, 10 to 15 minutes. Serve immediately.

Tip: Polenta will get fairly stiff once it cools. To restore its creamy consistency, reheat it over low heat and add water, broth, or unsweetened soy milk as necessary to thin it.

Cheesy Jalapeño Polenta: Add ½ cup of chopped pickled jalapeño chiles when you add the nutritional yeast.

Pesto Polenta: Add ⅓ cup Popeye Pesto (page 48) when you add the nutritional yeast.

Salsa Polenta: Add 1 cup of pico de gallo or tomatillo salsa when you add the nutritional yeast.

Per serving: 138 calories, 5 g protein, 1 g fat (0 g sat), 27 g carbohydrates, 310 mg sodium, 10 mg calcium, 6 g fiber

MAKES 4 SERVINGS

2 cups water
2 cups no-salt-added
    vegetable broth
½ teaspoon salt
1 cup coarsely ground
    yellow cornmeal
¼ cup nutritional yeast flakes

YOU MIGHT WANT to sit down when you read this recipe—it's that good. These are like French fries, but they're not. They're not French, they're not fried, and they're not even made from potatoes. I know, vegans are crazy!

Polenta Fries

MAKES 4 SERVINGS

1½ cups water
1½ cups no-salt-added
   vegetable broth
1 cup coarsely ground
   yellow cornmeal
¼ cup nutritional yeast flakes
½ teaspoon salt

PUT THE WATER and broth in a large saucepan and bring to a boil over medium-high heat. Slowly whisk in the cornmeal, stirring constantly. The polenta will thicken quickly and bubble (stand back to avoid splatters). Decrease the heat to low (keep stirring!) and stir in the nutritional yeast. Cover and cook, stirring frequently to prevent sticking, until the polenta is as thick as you like it, 10 to 15 minutes.

Mist a large rimmed baking sheet with cooking spray or line it with parchment paper.

Spread the polenta on the prepared baking sheet about ½ inch thick. Smooth the top. If the polenta has cooled enough, you can spread it with wet hands. Refrigerate for 1 to 12 hours or put in the freezer for 15 minutes.

When you're ready to bake the fries, preheat the oven to 450 degrees F. Cut the cold polenta into French-fry shapes or triangles or use a cookie cutter to make whatever shapes you like. Mist with cooking spray or brush lightly with olive oil and sprinkle with the salt. Bake for 25 minutes.

Per serving: 138 calories, 5 g protein, 1 g fat (0 g sat), 27 g carbohydrates, 310 mg sodium, 10 mg calcium, 6 g fiber

HERBIVORES HAVE A LOT of broccoli stalks to deal with. Sometimes I have an entire crisper drawer of them in my fridge! I dare not waste them, because waste not, want not, right? Here's a tip: broccoli stalks are a perfect substitute for celery in most dishes, especially cooked ones. They are also the star of the show in this recipe, though the real star just might be the simple but amazing sauce.

Ginger-Chili Broccoli Stalks

PUT THE CHILI SAUCE, hoisin sauce, tamari, sriracha sauce, and agave nectar in a small bowl and stir to combine.

Heat the oil in a large, heavy skillet (cast iron if you have one) over medium-high heat. When a drop of water sizzles in the skillet, you'll know the skillet is hot enough and ready. Add the broccoli stalks and stir to coat with the oil. Cook, stirring once or twice, until golden brown in spots, about 5 minutes. Add the ginger and garlic. Cook, stirring frequently, for 1 minute. Add the sauce and stir until the broccoli stalks are evenly coated. Cook for 1 minute.

Tip: If you don't have enough broccoli stalks, use celery to make up the difference. The dish will taste just as great. Crazy but true!

Per serving: 251 calories, 15 g protein, 11 g fat (2 g sat), 34 g carbohydrates, 659 mg sodium, 234 mg calcium, 1 g fiber

MAKES 2 SERVINGS

1 tablespoon sweet chili sauce
2 teaspoons hoisin sauce
2 teaspoons reduced-sodium tamari
1 teaspoon sriracha sauce
1 teaspoon agave nectar
1 tablespoon vegetable oil
1 tablespoon peeled and minced fresh ginger
2 teaspoons chopped garlic
4 cups broccoli stalks, peeled and cut into 2 x ½-inch sticks

I HOPE THAT TODAY'S kids aren't growing up like the kids of my youth did, thinking that eating Brussels sprouts was some sort of punishment. This recipe will set you up with a deliciously prepared sprout that will be a treat to eat. If the sprouts end up rolling too close to the gravy or mashed potatoes, or end up falling into a rice dish and getting covered with almost any sauce from this book, they will be even better for it.

Go-To Brussels Sprouts

MAKES 4 SERVINGS

1 pound Brussels sprouts, trimmed and halved if small or quartered if large
2 tablespoons olive oil
1 tablespoon reduced-sodium tamari
¼ teaspoon freshly ground black pepper

PREHEAT THE OVEN to 425 degrees F. Line a rimmed baking sheet with parchment paper.

Put the Brussels sprouts in a large bowl. Add the oil, tamari, and pepper and stir until evenly distributed. Arrange in a single layer on the lined baking sheet and bake for 25 minutes, tossing or turning the Brussels sprouts once to ensure even cooking.

Variation: Try any of the variations for Everyday Sweet Potato Fries (page 105).

Per serving: 104 calories, 4 g protein, 7 g fat (1 g sat), 8 g carbohydrates, 195 mg sodium, 50 mg calcium, 3 g fiber

GREEN BEANS ARE BORING. There. I said it. I have never cared about green beans or thought they were interesting or delicious. That is, until this recipe happened to green beans. Now I make these to snack on when there is leftover Peanut-Hoisin Sauce. What's happened to me?

Charred Green Beans with Peanut-Hoisin Sauce

MAKES 4 SERVINGS

1 teaspoon vegetable oil
1 pound green beans, trimmed
1 cup Peanut-Hoisin Sauce
   (page 62)

HEAT THE OIL in a large, heavy skillet (cast iron if you have one) over medium-high heat. When a drop of water sizzles in the skillet, you'll know the skillet is hot enough and ready. Add the green beans and cook, turning them just occasionally, until charred in spots but still crisp, about 8 minutes. Depending on the size of the skillet, you may need to do this in two batches. Transfer the green beans to a large bowl, add the sauce, and toss until evenly distributed. Snack away!

Per serving: 289 calories, 10 g protein, 17 g fat (2 g sat), 24 g carbohydrates, 377 mg sodium, 62 mg calcium, 6 g fiber

LET'S HEAR IT FOR THE quintessential summertime food: corn on the cob! Specifically, grilled corn on the cob. Ruby loves it plain (she's such a purist!), but this version is a grown-up favorite. Put the pesto in a pretty bowl with a spoon for serving at the table, and find a shaker for the Yellow Rose Parmesan. Let everyone shuck their own corn and dress their own cob. This is barbecue food, people!

Pesto-Parmesan Corn on the Cob

FIRE UP THE GRILL. When it's hot, grill the corn for 20 to 30 minutes, turning it two or three times to get all sides evenly cooked. Have a paper grocery sack ready. When the corn is done and has cooled a bit, let your family and friends shuck their own corn. Pass the paper sack around the table to collect the husks. At least that's how we do it. Smother the corn in pesto, then cover with Yellow Rose Parmesan. Devour.

Tip: If it's raining or sleeting or you don't have a grill, you can boil the corn instead. Shuck the corn first, then bring a large pot of water to a rolling boil. Add the corn and cook for about 3 minutes. Boiling corn for too long will make it tough.

Per serving: 223 calories, 7 g protein, 9 g fat (1 g sat), 34 g carbohydrates, 226 mg sodium, 17 mg calcium, 5 g fiber

MAKES 4 SERVINGS

4 ears corn, with husk, soaked in water for 1 hour
¼ cup Popeye Pesto (page 48)
¼ cup Yellow Rose Parmesan (page 50)

THIS IS PERHAPS THE simplest dish in the book, and we wondered if it was silly to even include it. Then we gave it the test: Did Josh know how to cook greens when he went vegan? The answer came back a resounding no. There is no shame if you don't know how to cook greens. Soon you will! Wash the greens well but don't dry them; the water on their leaves will help them steam. Most greens reduce quite a bit when cooked. Below are the average amounts and cooking times we use for our favorite types of greens.

Go-To Greens

MAKES 4 SERVINGS

Baby spinach: 1 bag (5 ounces). No prep or washing needed. Steam-fry for 4 minutes.

Collard greens: 1 bunch (6 to 8 leaves), cleaned, stemmed, and coarsely chopped. Steam-fry for 15 to 20 minutes.

Kale: 1 bunch (8 to 10 leaves), cleaned, stemmed, and coarsely chopped. Steam-fry for 6 to 8 minutes.

Swiss chard: 1 bunch (5 or 6 very large leaves, or 12 to 15 small leaves), cleaned, stemmed (save the stems if you like), and coarsely chopped. Steam-fry the leaves for 5 minutes. If you like the stems, dice them and steam-fry them for 5 minutes before adding the leaves.

TO STEAM-FRY GREENS, put $\frac{1}{4}$ cup of water or broth in a large, deep skillet or saucepan. Add the greens and bring to a boil over medium-high heat. Cook, stirring almost constantly, until the greens are tender to your liking. Add more water or broth if needed to prevent sticking or burning.

Serving suggestion: There are lots of ways to eat greens other than straight up. You can top them with Tahini Sauce (page 45), chop them finely and add them to a rice or noodle bowl, tuck them into a quesadilla, or toss them with pasta and your favorite sauce.

CONFESSION TIME. When I'm making something with canned chickpeas, Josh will eat at least one-third of them before the rest make it into the dish. He loves plain chickpeas so much that it's a miracle we ever get around to making anything with them. These are great in salads and rice bowls, or you can just pop 'em in your mouth as a snack (like Josh does).

Skillet Chickpeas

HEAT THE OIL IN a heavy skillet (cast iron if you have one) over medium heat. When hot, add the chickpeas and shake the skillet briefly to distribute the oil. Cook, shaking the skillet occasionally, until the chickpeas are brown and crispy on all sides, 12 to 15 minutes. Sprinkle the za'atar over the chickpeas and shake the skillet or stir well to combine.

Variation: In place of the za'atar, use chili powder, nutritional yeast flakes, or any other seasoning blend to taste. You could also replace the za'atar with barbecue sauce.

Per serving: 157 calories, 6 g protein, 4 g fat (1 g sat), 18 g carbohydrates, 26 mg sodium, 53 mg calcium, 5 g fiber

MAKES 4 SERVINGS

1 tablespoon olive oil
1 can (15 ounces) no-salt added
   chickpeas, rinsed and drained
2 tablespoons za'atar
   (see page 11)

EATING THIS LENTIL DISH makes me feel as though I'm vacationing in the French countryside, wearing my beret and sipping red wine. It must be the aroma: earthy lentils; tart, sun-dried tomatoes; good vinegar; and fresh herbs. The combination of flavors will make a lentil lover out of anyone. French lentils are perfect here, as they hold their shape so well.

Lentils with Sun-Dried Tomatoes

PUT THE LENTILS and broth in a large saucepan and bring to a boil over high heat. Stir, decrease the heat to medium, cover, and cook until tender, 25 to 30 minutes. Don't overcook!

While the lentils are cooking, put the onion, vinegar, and salt in a large bowl and stir to combine. The vinegar and salt will help soften the onion. Sprinkle the parsley, chives, sun-dried tomatoes, thyme, and garlic over the top but don't stir. (This will keep the onion marinating underneath the seasonings while the lentils cook.)

When the lentils are done, drain them well and add them to the bowl with the onion along with the olive oil. Stir gently to combine. Season with pepper to taste and stir again. Serve immediately, at room temperature, or chilled.

Variation: To turn this salad into a main dish, add cooked grain or pasta and an additional tablespoon of olive oil.

Serving suggestion: Spoon the salad over baby lettuce leaves.

Per serving: 227 calories, 13 g protein, 10 g fat (1 g sat), 35 g carbohydrates, 623 mg sodium, 13 mg calcium, 14 g fiber

MAKES 4 SERVINGS

1½ cups dried French lentils or green lentils, rinsed and drained
2½ cups no-salt-added vegetable broth
½ cup finely chopped red onion
2 tablespoons balsamic vinegar
1 teaspoon salt
¼ cup chopped fresh parsley
¼ cup chopped fresh chives or scallions
¼ cup sliced sun-dried tomatoes (preferably not packed in oil)
2 tablespoons fresh thyme, or 1 teaspoon dried
1 teaspoon chopped garlic
3 tablespoons olive oil
Freshly ground black pepper

EVERYONE'S MOM HAS some kind of bean "caviar" recipe, right? Usually it's named after a Southern state, as in "Texas caviar" or "Louisiana caviar." This appears to be a way to make bean salads seem fancy. I don't care, because pretty much all of them are fabulous, perfect for a pot-luck, picnic, or a big group of friends with a couple of bags of corn chips. My mom makes about a gallon of this every time we visit, and I'm not exaggerating.

Oma's Full of Beans

MAKES 5 CUPS

2 cups pico de gallo
1 can (15 ounces) black eyed
    peas, rinsed and drained
1 can (15 ounces) white hominy,
    rinsed and drained
1 yellow or orange bell
    pepper, diced
½ cup diced white onion
½ cup chopped scallions
⅓ cup chopped fresh cilantro
1 jalapeño chile, seeded
    and diced
1 tablespoon hot sauce
1 tablespoon agave nectar
2 teaspoons ground cumin
½ teaspoon salt
¼ teaspoon freshly ground
    black pepper

PUT ALL THE INGREDIENTS in a large bowl and stir to combine. Cover and refrigerate for at least 1 hour before serving so the flavors can blend.

Variation: Mash and heat in a skillet and serve as a taco filling.

Per cup: 149 calories, 5 g protein, 2 g fat (0 g sat), 29 g carbohydrates, 809 mg sodium, 36 mg calcium, 7 g fiber

especially since our recipes always include plenty of greens and other veggies. Our version of a decadent burger is packed with vegetables masquerading as meat and served on a whole-grain bun with a side of homemade pickles. If we invite you to dinner at our house, you'll likely be served something from this chapter. We've created this magical stash of classic foods—all cruelty-free, all filling and delicious—along with some super-simple dishes that are natural vegan all-stars. Turns out, we vegans are wizards at veganizing just about anything.

Mains

Fubonn Bowls, Page 150

I MAKE THESE WANNA-BE ravioli pretty often because they're darned good. It may seem like a fussy recipe, but it's actually really easy and fun. Make the pesto sauce while the potatoes and garlic are roasting, and round up whoever is eating with you to help make the ravioli. We tend to crowd around the stove and eat these in batches as soon as they're ready.

Sweet Potato Ravioli with Popeye Pesto Sauce

MAKES 20 RAVIOLI, 4 SERVINGS

Ravioli Filling
2 large sweet potatoes, scrubbed
8 large garlic cloves, peeled
1 tablespoon plus 1 teaspoon olive oil
1 teaspoon rubbed sage
¼ teaspoon freshly ground black pepper
Pinch cayenne

Ravioli
1 package (12 ounces) vegan wonton wrappers

Popeye Pesto Sauce
½ cup Popeye Pesto (page 48)
¼ cup no-salt-added vegetable broth

Garnish
Yellow Rose Parmesan (page 50)

PREHEAT THE OVEN to 400 degrees F. Line a baking sheet with parchment paper.

To make filling, put the sweet potatoes on the lined baking sheet. Tear a piece of aluminum foil about 8 inches long to make a packet for the garlic. Put the garlic on the foil and sprinkle with 1 teaspoon of the oil. Bring the sides of the foil up to make a little purse and keep the oil from leaking out. Put the packet on the baking sheet with the sweet potatoes. Bake the sweet potatoes and garlic for 30 minutes. Remove the garlic from the oven and set aside to cool. Continue baking the sweet potatoes for 20 to 30 minutes longer, until easily pierced with a fork. Let the sweet potatoes cool until they can be easily handled. Decrease the oven temperature to 200 degrees F.

Peel the sweet potatoes, mash the flesh, and measure out 3 cups (save any leftovers for another recipe) and put in a food processor. Add the garlic, remaining tablespoon of oil, and the sage, pepper, and cayenne. Process until creamy, about 1 minute.

Fill a small bowl with water. Dampen a clean kitchen towel or paper towels to cover the finished ravioli as you make them (otherwise, they'll dry out). Put one wrapper on a flat surface and put 1 tablespoon of the filling in the center. Take another wrapper, dampen your fingers with the water in the small bowl, and run your fingers around the perimeter of the wrapper to moisten it. Put the moistened wrapper over the wrapper with the filling

(moist-side down) and press gently to seal all four sides together. The water will act as glue. Put the ravioli under the damp towel. Continue in the same fashion until all the wrappers have been used. If you have leftover filling, store it in the refrigerator for a snack. Yum!

To cook the ravioli, mist a large nonstick or cast iron skillet with cooking spray and heat over medium heat. Gently put the ravioli in the pan and cook until golden, about 2 minutes per side. Sprinkle 1 tablespoon of water over the ravioli before removing them from the skillet. Transfer to a baking pan, cover loosely with foil, and put in the oven to keep warm.

To make the sauce, put the pesto in a small saucepan. Whisk in the broth until smooth. Heat over medium heat until hot.

To serve, put the ravioli on a plate and pour the sauce evenly over them. Garnish with Yellow Rose Parmesan.

Per serving: 386 calories, 8 g protein, 23 g fat (3 g sat), 38 g carbohydrates, 714 mg sodium, 62 mg calcium, 4 g fiber

Note: Analysis doesn't include Yellow Rose Parmesan to garnish.

THIS IS RESTAURANT-STYLE macaroni and cheese because it's the seriously decadent kind, just like restaurants serve, but vegan. People who say they can't go vegan because they would miss cheese too much need to try this recipe. Vegans are deprived? Ha!

Restaurant-Style Baked Macaroni and Cheese

COOK THE MACARONI in boiling water according to the package directions. Drain and cover to keep warm.

Preheat the oven to 325 degrees F. Mist a 13 x 9-inch casserole dish with cooking spray or lightly coat with vegetable oil.

To make the sauce, put the Cashew Cream and vegetable broth in a small saucepan and whisk to combine. Heat over medium heat, whisking frequently, until just starting to bubble, about 5 minutes. Add the cheese, whisking constantly. Once the cheese is melted, whisk in the nutritional yeast until well combined.

To assemble, transfer the macaroni to the prepared casserole dish. Pour the cheese sauce over it and stir until evenly coated. Sprinkle the Parmesan evenly over the top, cover tightly with foil, and bake for 15 minutes. Remove the foil and bake for 10 minutes longer.

Variation: Add bite-sized broccoli florets to the casserole dish when you combine the macaroni and the cheese sauce. A dash or two of hot sauce would also be a welcome addition.

Per serving: 309 calories, 19 g protein, 11 g fat (12 g sat), 26 g carbohydrates, 368 mg sodium, 6 mg calcium, 3 g fiber

MAKES 6 SERVINGS

1 pound macaroni, pasta shells, rigatoni, or penne
1 cup Cashew Cream (page 56)
1 cup no-salt-added vegetable broth
1 cup shredded vegan Cheddar cheese
½ cup nutritional yeast flakes
½ cup Yellow Rose Parmesan (page 50)

POT PIE WAS ONE OF the first dishes I wanted to veganize the winter after I stopped eating animals. That first cold and rainy day, I was dreaming about it. I've never enjoyed making crusts, though. So my genius solution was to top the pie with biscuits, which are simple to make. This is a straight-up American-style pot pie, but with a few more vegetables.

Hungry Vegan Pot Pie

MAKES 6 SERVINGS

1 tablespoon olive oil, plus more for brushing the biscuits
1 cup finely chopped onion
3 large garlic cloves, minced
1 cup diced carrot
1 cup chopped celery
1 cup peeled and diced parsnip
1 cup peeled and diced potato
1 cup fresh or frozen peas
¾ cup fresh or frozen corn kernels
2 teaspoons poultry seasoning
½ teaspoon dried thyme
⅓ cup unbleached all-purpose flour or other flour
2 tablespoons white wine or cooking sherry
1 cup no-salt-added vegetable broth
2 cups unsweetened soy milk
1 cup finely chopped broccoli florets
Freshly ground pepper
Salt
1 recipe Cream Biscuits (page 22), unbaked, dough shaped into 10 biscuits

PREHEAT THE OVEN to 425 degrees F. Lightly oil a 13 x 9-inch baking dish or mist with cooking spray.

Put the oil in a large, heavy saucepan and heat over medium heat. When hot, add the onion and garlic and cook, stirring almost constantly, for 3 minutes. Add the carrot, celery, parsnip, and potato and cook, stirring frequently, for 5 minutes. Add the peas and corn and cook, stirring frequently, for 3 minutes. Add the poultry seasoning and thyme and stir to combine. Sprinkle the flour over the vegetables and stir well to combine. Deglaze the saucepan with the wine, scraping up any bits stuck on the bottom. Stir in the vegetable broth and cook, stirring almost constantly, for 2 minutes. Stir in the soy milk. Increase the heat to medium-high and bring to a boil, stirring frequently. Remove from the heat. Stir in the broccoli and season with salt and pepper to taste.

Pour the vegetable mixture into the prepared baking dish. Bake for 15 minutes. Remove from the oven and arrange the biscuits evenly over the top. Brush the biscuits lightly with oil. Bake for 15 to 20 minutes, until the biscuits are browned and the filling is bubbly.

Variation: For an even heartier pot pie, add 1 cup of cooked chickpeas or 1 cup of chopped chicken-style seitan to the vegetable mixture before pouring it into the baking dish.

Per serving: 356 calories, 14 g protein, 8 g fat (3 g sat), 61 g carbohydrates, 378 mg sodium, 206 mg calcium, 9 g fiber

Note: Analysis doesn't include salt to taste.

EVERYTHING ABOUT THESE burgers is delicious. We've fine-tuned them that way through months of enjoyable recipe testing. Roasting the vegetables and tofu makes them taste incredible, and beets make the meatiest-looking veggie burger ever. There is no need to chop the vegetables uniformly or in small pieces, because you'll be using a food processor to make the ground "meat," so the prep work is super easy.

Roasted Beet Burgers

PREHEAT THE OVEN to 400 degrees F. Line a baking sheet with parchment paper.

Put the mushrooms, beet, onion, and garlic in a large bowl. Using your hands, crumble the tofu into the bowl, making sure to break up the pieces well, and stir to combine. Add the oil, tamari, and thyme and mix well. Spread the mixture on the lined baking sheet so it covers the whole sheet. Bake for 20 minutes. Stir and spread out the mixture again. Bake for 25 minutes longer, until the beet is tender and easily pierced with a fork. Remove from the oven and let cool slightly.

Transfer to a food processor. Add the quinoa, nutritional yeast, salt, and pepper. Pulse eight to ten times, stopping occasionally to scrape down the work bowl, until all the ingredients are well chopped and stick together. Return the mixture to the large bowl. Form into 6 patties, putting each patty on waxed paper as it's shaped.

Mist a large skillet (cast iron if you have one) with cooking spray and heat over medium heat. When hot, cook the patties until crispy (in batches, if necessary), about 5 minutes per side.

Tip: Use a beet about the size of a baseball. Scrub it well so you can leave the skin on.

Per burger: 204 calories, 14 g protein, 10 g fat (2 g sat), 16 g carbohydrates, 491 mg sodium, 253 mg calcium, 4 g fiber

MAKES 6 BURGERS

2 cups quartered crimini mushrooms

$1\frac{1}{2}$ cups coarsely chopped beet (see tip)

$\frac{1}{3}$ cup coarsely chopped onion

4 large cloves garlic, coarsely chopped

1 pound super-firm or extra-firm tofu, drained and pressed (see page 12)

2 tablespoons olive oil

2 tablespoons reduced-sodium tamari

2 teaspoons dried thyme

1 cup cooked quinoa, farro, or brown rice

$\frac{1}{4}$ cup nutritional yeast flakes

$\frac{1}{2}$ teaspoon salt

$\frac{1}{4}$ teaspoon freshly ground black pepper

PREPARING HOMEMADE pizza dough is a magical experience, and it makes this cultural train wreck of deliciousness all the more special. But it's fine to use a store-bought crust, if you prefer. Look for a cornmeal crust for the best results, but any crust that's vegan will do. If you're like us, you love leftover pizza for breakfast. If you're like us, you'll never see any of this left over, because it's so damn good.

Skillet Taco Pizza

MAKES 8 SLICES

½ recipe Cornmeal Pizza Crust (page 80), unbaked
Cornmeal, for dusting
1 cup fresh or thawed frozen corn
½ cup finely chopped white onion
2 large cloves garlic, minced
½ teaspoon chili powder
½ cup thick salsa
1 cup refried beans
1 cup Tofu Queso Fresco (page 53)
1 avocado, diced
¼ cup chopped fresh cilantro

PREHEAT THE OVEN to 475 degrees F. Mist a 10- or 12-inch cast iron skillet or other oven-safe skillet with cooking spray and dust with cornmeal. The pizza pan is ready.

Mist a medium skillet with cooking spray and heat over medium heat. When hot, add the corn, onion, garlic, and chili powder and cook, stirring frequently, until the corn and onion brown and smell divine, 5 to 10 minutes. Set aside.

Roll out the pizza dough to one inch wider than the circumference of the prepared skillet. Lay the dough in the skillet and gently press it down. The dough should come up the sides of the skillet a bit. This will create a great pizza-eating handle. Woo!

Spread the salsa over the dough. Spread the refried beans over the salsa. If the beans are thick, don't worry. Just put a dollop down and spread it out as best you can; the oven will do the rest. Sprinkle the corn mixture evenly over the refried beans. Drop spoonfuls of the Tofu Queso Fresco over the top (remember that it will melt and spread in the oven too).

Bake for 12 minutes. Check to see if the crust is done to your liking. Bake for 1 to 2 minutes longer if it's not yet done. Cast iron gets very hot, so take care not to burn the crust (or your hand—wear an oven mitt!). When the pizza is done, it will easily turn out onto a cutting board in one piece. Top with the avocado and sprinkle with the cilantro. Cut the pie into slices and enjoy!

Per slice: 240 calories, 10 g protein, 9 g fat (1 g sat), 30 g carbohydrates, 435 mg sodium, 94 mg calcium, 6 g fiber

Note: Analysis doesn't include cornmeal for dusting.

WHEN JOSH AND I first met, he had been vegan for all of two weeks and I was an omnivore. We always wanted to eat out on our dates, but in 1999, vegan options at restaurants were much harder to find. So we ended up cooking together quite a bit instead. These easy-as-can-be pizzas were one of our favorites back then, and we still love them.

First-Date Pita Pizzas

PREHEAT THE OVEN to 400 degrees F. Line a rimmed baking sheet with parchment paper.

Put the oil, garlic, vinegar, and salt in a small bowl and stir to combine.

Mist a skillet (cast iron if you have one) with cooking spray and heat over medium heat. Add the spinach and cook, stirring frequently, until wilted, about 3 minutes.

Spread one-quarter of the oil mixture over one side of each pita bread, making sure to distribute the garlic evenly. Next, distribute the spinach, walnuts, cherries, and feta in that order equally over the pita breads. Arrange on the lined baking sheet. Bake for 8 minutes, just until heated through.

Per pizza: 515 calories, 16 g protein, 32 g fat (3 g sat), 48 g carbohydrates, 462 mg sodium, 150 mg calcium, 4 g fiber

MAKES 4 PIZZAS

2 tablespoons olive oil
1 tablespoon minced garlic
1 teaspoon balsamic vinegar
Pinch salt
2 cups chopped spinach, packed
4 pita breads
¼ cup walnuts
⅓ cup dried cherries, chopped
1 cup So Faux Feta (page 47)

JOSH GREW UP IN a Southern family, so eating cheese grits with hot sauce is totally his thing, and I think polenta deserves more attention at the dining tables of America. So here we have spicy, cheesy polenta with humble vegetables and beans, which makes a comfort food that's both tasty and nutritious.

Cheesy Polenta with Mushrooms, Swiss Chard, and Pinto Beans

MAKES 4 SERVINGS

Cheesy Tomatillo Polenta

2 cups water
2 cups no-salt-added
   vegetable broth
1 cup coarsely ground
   yellow cornmeal
¼ cup nutritional yeast flakes
1 cup tomatillo salsa or other
   mild green salsa

Mushroom, Swiss Chard, and Pinto Bean Sauté

1 tablespoon olive oil
2 cups sliced crimini
   mushrooms
1 teaspoon dried oregano
1½ cups chopped onions
1 cup chopped poblano chiles
2 tablespoons minced garlic
1 can (15 ounces) no-salt added
   pinto beans, rinsed
   and drained
1 tablespoon chili powder
1 teaspoon ground cumin
4 cups stemmed and chopped
   Swiss chard leaves
Salt
Freshly ground black pepper
¼ cup pumpkin seeds, toasted
   (see tip) and chopped

TO MAKE THE POLENTA, put the water and broth in a large saucepan and bring to a boil over medium-high heat. Slowly whisk in the cornmeal, stirring constantly. The polenta will thicken quickly and bubble (stand back to avoid splatters). Decrease the heat to low (keep stirring!) and stir in the nutritional yeast and salsa. Cover and cook, stirring frequently to prevent sticking, until the polenta is as thick as you like it, 10 to 15 minutes.

To make the sauté, put 1½ teaspoons of the oil in a large, heavy skillet (cast iron if you have one) and heat over medium heat. When hot, add the mushrooms and cook, stirring frequently, for 2 minutes. Add the oregano and stir to combine. Cook, stirring frequently, until the mushrooms release their juices and most of the liquid has evaporated, about 3 minutes longer. Transfer the mushrooms to a bowl and set aside.

Put the remaining 1½ teaspoons of oil in the skillet and heat over medium heat. When hot, add the onions, chiles, and garlic. Cook, stirring frequently, until the onions start to brown, about 6 minutes. Add the beans, chili powder, and cumin and stir to mix well. Stir in the Swiss chard, cover, and cook for 3 minutes. Stir in the reserved mushrooms. Season with salt and pepper to taste.

To serve, spoon the polenta onto plates, top with the vegetable mixture, and sprinkle with the pumpkin seeds.

Tip: To toast the pumpkin seeds, heat a small skillet over medium-high heat. When hot, add the pumpkin seeds and toast, stirring frequently, until they turn a shade or two darker and are fragrant, 3 to 4 minutes. To keep the seeds from burning, remove from the heat immediately and transfer to a plate to cool.

Per serving: 339 calories, 16 g protein, 7 g fat (1 g sat), 55 g carbohydrates, 624 mg sodium, 98 mg calcium, 16 g fiber

Note: Analysis doesn't include salt to taste.

THIS IS WHAT YOU'LL want to make for your very first vegan Thanksgiving dinner, and every Thanksgiving dinner after that too. It's hearty comfort food with all the best flavors of the season. Serve it with the usual trimmings and you'll be more thankful than ever that you went vegan.

Portobello-Chickpea Wellington

PREHEAT THE OVEN to 400 degrees F. Line a baking sheet with parchment paper.

Put the chickpeas, walnuts, breadcrumbs, and nutritional yeast in a food processor and pulse until coarsely chopped. Don't overprocess or the filling will be mushy.

Heat a large, heavy skillet (cast iron if you have one) over medium-high heat. When hot, add the mushrooms and onion and cook, stirring frequently, for 5 minutes. Add the garlic and thyme and cook, stirring frequently, for 2 minutes. Deglaze the pan with the wine and scrape and mix in any brown bits from the the bottom of the skillet. Continue to cook, stirring frequently, until most of the liquid has evaporated, 5 to 7 minutes. Add the chickpea mixture, corn, peas, and parsley and stir until well combined. Season with salt and pepper to taste. Stir well to bind the mixture together. Remove from the heat and let cool.

Lightly flour a flat surface and roll out one sheet of the puff pastry to make a 14 x 12-inch rectangle. Spoon half the chickpea mixture onto the pastry and form it into a loaf, pressing the mixture lightly. Wrap the puff pastry around the loaf and tuck and seal the edges like a wrapped present. Repeat with the other sheet of puff pastry and the remaining chickpea mixture. Put the loaves seam-side down on the prepared baking sheet. Make five angled 3-inch slashes on the top of each loaf with a sharp knife to allow steam to escape. Mist the top of each loaf with cooking spray or brush with a little olive oil so it browns.

Bake for 25 to 30 minutes, until the pastry is golden brown. Let cool for 5 minutes before slicing.

Tip: Pepperidge Farm brand puff pastry is vegan.

Per serving: 487 calories, 15 g protein, 15 g fat (6 g sat), 49 g carbohydrates, 215 mg sodium, 83 mg calcium, 7 g fiber

MAKES 2 ROASTS, 8 SERVINGS (4 SERVINGS PER ROAST)

1 can (15 ounces) no-salt-added chickpeas, rinsed and drained
1¼ cups chopped walnuts, toasted (see tip, page 87)
1¼ cups fresh breadcrumbs
¼ cup nutritional yeast flakes
2 cups diced cremini mushrooms
1 cup finely chopped onion
4 cloves garlic, minced
1 teaspoon dried thyme
¼ cup white wine, sherry, or no-salt-added vegetable broth
½ cup fresh or frozen corn
½ cup fresh or frozen peas
¼ cup chopped fresh parsley
Salt
Freshly ground black pepper
1 package (1 pound) vegan puff pastry (see tip), thawed per package instructions

ALTHOUGH THIS RECIPE makes twelve enchiladas, Josh likes to think that's a single serving. Between the delicious sauce, sweet plantains, and yummy beans, this dish is a winner, even if you have to share it. In fact, these enchiladas are perfect for potlucks or dinner parties.

Black Bean, Mushroom, and Plaintain Enchiladas

MAKES 12 ENCHILADAS, 6 SERVINGS

Enchilada Sauce (makes 3 cups)
½ cup unbleached all purpose flour or other flour
¼ cup New Mexico or regular chili powder
1 tablespoon unsweetened cocoa powder (if using regular chili powder, add an additional tablespoon of cocoa powder)
2 teaspoons garlic granules
1 teaspoon ground cumin
½ teaspoon dried oregano
4 cups no-salt-added vegetable broth
1 tablespoon agave nectar

Filling
2 tablespoons vegetable oil
1 ripe plantain (skin should be at least 50 percent black), peeled and sliced into quarters
1 cup finely chopped white onion
1½ cups chopped crimini mushrooms
1 teaspoon ground cumin
½ teaspoon dried oregano
½ teaspoon salt
1 can (15 ounces) black beans, rinsed and drained
1 tablespoon chopped garlic
¼ cup chopped fresh cilantro
12 small corn or flour tortillas
⅓ cup shredded vegan cheese (optional)

TO MAKE THE SAUCE, put the flour, chili powder, cocoa powder, garlic granules, cumin, and oregano in a medium saucepan and whisk to combine. Slowly whisk in the broth until smooth and lump-free. Bring to a boil over medium heat, whisking occasionally to avoid lumps and sticking. Decrease the heat to medium-low and cook, whisking frequently, until the sauce thickens, about 5 minutes. Remove from the heat and stir in the agave nectar.

Preheat the oven to 350 degrees F. Mist a 13 x 9-inch baking dish with cooking spray.

To make the filling, put 1 tablespoon of the oil in a large, heavy skillet (cast iron if you have one) and heat over medium heat. When hot, add the plantain and cook, turning once, until brown and crispy on both sides, about 5 minutes per side. As

the plantain quarters cook, flatten them a bit with a metal spatula to create more surface area to brown. Transfer to a plate and let cool. When cool, chop into bite-sized pieces.

Add the remaining tablespoon of oil to the skillet and heat over medium heat. When hot, add the onion and cook, stirring frequently, for 1 minute. Add the mushrooms, cumin, oregano, and salt and stir to combine. Cook, stirring frequently, until the mushrooms release their juices and most of the liquid has evaporated, about 6 minutes. Add the beans and garlic and cook, stirring occasionally, for 2 minutes. Remove from the heat and stir in the cilantro and plantains.

To assemble the enchiladas, spread ½ cup of the enchilada sauce evenly in the prepared baking dish. Spoon ⅓ cup of the filling on each tortilla

and wrap the tortillas around the filling. Put the enchiladas in the baking dish seam-side down. Top with the remaining enchilada sauce, sprinkle with the optional vegan cheese, and cover tightly with foil. Bake for 20 minutes. Remove the foil and bake for 5 minutes longer.

Tip: If you're feeding people who think they don't like mushrooms, just chop the mushrooms extra small. They'll be unrecognizable once they're mixed with the other ingredients.

Per 2 enchiladas: 384 calories, 9 g protein, 9 g fat (1 g sat), 68 g carbohydrates, 360 mg sodium, 65 mg calcium, 9 g fiber

PANCAKES FOR DINNER? Heck yeah! But we are savory-breakfast types, too, so these pancakes are perfect any hour of the day. This recipe, influenced by the cuisine of South India, is endlessly adaptable (add whatever veggies you like!) and very filling. We often use two skillets and cook both pancakes at the same time. Then we slice them like pizza.

Savory Chickpea Pancakes

PUT THE FLOUR, garlic granules, onion granules, turmeric, salt, and baking soda in a medium bowl and whisk to combine. Add the water a little bit at a time and stir with a silicone spatula, breaking up any clumps of flour. Scrape the bowl as needed and continue mixing for about 1 minute until smooth. Add the onion, peas, and tomato and stir until evenly distributed. Stir in the lemon juice and mix well. Let sit until you see a few bubbles in the batter, about 5 minutes. That means it's time to cook these pancakes!

Oil a large, heavy skillet (cast iron if you have one) or mist with cooking spray and heat over medium heat. When hot, pour half the batter into the skillet, making sure to include half the vegetables. Cook until well browned on the bottom, about 8 minutes. Flip and cook the other side until well browned, about 8 minutes longer. As it cooks, the pancake will puff up to almost an inch thick.

Tip: Preheat the oven to 200 degrees F. Put the first pancake on an ovenproof plate and put it in the oven to keep warm while you cook the second pancake.

Variation: For four small pancakes (instead of two large ones), use a smaller skillet and cook the pancakes in four batches.

Serving suggestion: Serve with a spoonful of unsweetened vegan yogurt, store-bought vegan sour cream, or Cashew Cream (page 56), and a spicy chutney or relish.

Per large pancake: 374 calories, 21 g protein, 6 g fat (0 g sat), 71 g carbohydrates, 373 mg sodium, 148 mg calcium, 19 g fiber

MAKES 2 LARGE PANCAKES

1½ cups chickpea flour (see page 10)
1 teaspoon garlic granules
1 teaspoon onion granules
¼ teaspoon ground turmeric
1 teaspoon salt
½ teaspoon baking soda
¾ cup water
½ cup diced onion
½ cup fresh or thawed frozen peas
½ cup chopped tomato
1 tablespoon lemon juice

AS YOU MAY HAVE HEARD, our beloved hometown of Portland, Oregon, gets a little bit of rain. And in the winter, this rain is combined with short, dark days, resulting in an ever-present chilliness that creates the perfect storm for big bowls of warm comfort food. This one, with barbecue sauce and the hauntingly meaty texture of Soy Curls, is sure to warm you up, especially if you lean toward the spicy side of life (or sauce).

Curry-Barbecue Soy Curls Bowls

MAKES 4 SERVINGS

Vegan Meat
3 cups Butler Soy Curls (see page 11)
4 cups boiling water
1 teaspoon no-salt-added vegan bouillon powder, or 1 no-salt-added vegan bouillon cube
1 cup barbecue sauce
2 teaspoons maple syrup (optional)
1 teaspoon curry powder

Veggies
8 leaves collard greens, stemmed and coarsely chopped
1 cup fresh or thawed frozen corn kernels

Rice and Topping
4 cups cooked brown rice, hot
1 cup Don't-Be-Blue Cheese Dressing (page 44)

TO MAKE THE VEGAN meat, put the Soy Curls in a large bowl. Add the water and bouillon powder and let soak for 10 minutes, Drain, reserving ½ cup of the soaking liquid.

Put the barbecue sauce, optional maple syrup, and curry powder in a medium saucepan and stir to combine. Bring to a boil over medium-high heat. Decrease the heat to medium, add the Soy Curls, and stir to coat. Partially cover and cook, stirring occasionally, for 20 minutes.

To make the veggies, put the collard greens and reserved soaking liquid in a large saucepan. Cover and cook over medium heat, stirring occasionally, for 15 minutes. Add the corn and cook until the collard greens are tender but not mushy, about 5 minutes longer.

To serve, divide the rice, veggies, and vegan meat (in that order) equally among four bowls. Drizzle the dressing over the top.

Tip: If you can't find Butler Soy Curls, use 1 pound of your favorite vegan chicken, sliced. The vegan chicken can be added directly to the sauce mixture (no soaking is needed). Replace the soaking liquid for the collard greens with ½ cup of water.

Per serving: 673 calories, 22 g protein, 24 g fat (4 g sat), 92 g carbohydrates, 1,041 mg sodium, 101 mg calcium, 11 g fiber

THIS COLORFUL, NUTRIENT-DENSE dish has been in heavy rotation at our house for a long time. It seems almost too simple to count as a recipe, but the flavors and textures work together so perfectly that we couldn't resist sharing it with you. We always go back for seconds. Josh usually goes for thirds.

Herbivore Bowls

MAKES 4 SERVINGS

3 cups peeled and cubed sweet potatoes

10 cups stemmed and chopped curly kale

6 cups cooked quinoa, hot

1 can (15 ounces) no-salt added black beans, rinsed, drained, and warmed

1 cup Tahini Sauce (page 45)

PUT 2 INCHES OF water in a large soup pot fitted with a steamer basket. Put the sweet potatoes in the steamer and heat over medium-high heat until a good head of steam forms. Cover and cook for 5 minutes. Put the kale on top of the sweet potatoes, cover, and cook for 2 minutes. Remove from the heat and let sit, covered, for 1 minute to finish steaming the kale. Using tongs, transfer the kale to a medium bowl. Put the sweet potatoes in a separate bowl. Cover both bowls to keep warm.

Now you're ready to build the bowls. Divide the quinoa, beans, sweet potatoes, and kale (in that order) evenly among four bowls. Drizzle the sauce over the top.

Per serving: 714 calories, 29 g protein, 7 g fat (3 g sat), 116 g carbohydrates, 310 mg sodium, 354 mg calcium, 21 g fiber

WE ARE BIG FANS OF Middle Eastern food and have been fortunate enough to travel to Beirut, Lebanon. One of the many things we discovered there is the allure of the ubiquitous spice blend called za'atar. Za'atar can be purchased at Middle Eastern grocery stores and from online retailers. It's most often mixed with olive oil and used as a topping on flatbread called man'oushe, but za'atar also makes the beans in this bowl taste amazing.

Beirut Bowls

PUT THE OIL IN A large, heavy skillet (cast iron if you have one) over medium heat. When hot, add the chickpeas and shake briefly to distribute the oil. Cook, shaking the skillet occasionally, until the chickpeas are evenly browned, 12 to 15 minutes. Sprinkle the za'atar over the chickpeas and stir. Pour the water in the center and stir to combine. Immediately transfer the chickpeas to a plate.

Put the hot skillet over medium heat. Put all the Swiss chard in the skillet and cover. The Swiss chard should sizzle a bit and immediately start to steam and wilt. It won't take long to cook! After 1 minute, lift the lid and give the leaves a stir. The moisture should loosen the little bits of za'atar stuck on the bottom of the skillet, making the Swiss chard even tastier. Cook covered until all the leaves are wilted, about 1 minute longer. Remove from the heat and keep covered.

To serve, divide the farro, chickpeas, Swiss chard, tomatoes, onion, olives, and avocado (in that order) equally among four bowls or plates. Drizzle the sauce evenly over the top. Garnish with a sprinkle of additional za'atar.

Per serving: 520 calories, 24 g protein, 22 g fat (3 g sat), 106 g carbohydrates, 541 mg sodium, 126 mg calcium, 22 g fiber

MAKES 4 SERVINGS

1 tablespoon olive oil
1 can (15 ounces) no-salt-added chickpeas, rinsed and drained
1½ tablespoons za'atar (see page 11), plus more for garnish
2 tablespoons water
6 large or 12 small Swiss chard leaves, stemmed and chopped
5 cups cooked farro, hot
1½ cups chopped tomatoes
½ cup minced red onion
½ cup pitted and quartered kalamata olives
½ cup diced avocado
1 cup Tahini Sauce (page 45)

FOR THIS RECIPE, common plant ingredients are transformed into what is usually a meaty affair. If you love a good reuben sandwich, try this out. If you were a fan of corned beef before you became vegan, this is for you. If you love sauerkraut, come and get it! You can also serve this burger on rye bread, if you're a purist, or add a slice of vegan cheese, if you dare.

Corned Bean Burgers with Sauerkraut

MAKES 4 BURGERS

Smoky Thousand Island Dressing (makes ¾ cup)
½ cup vegan mayonnaise
2 tablespoons sweet pickle relish
2 tablespoons ketchup
1 teaspoon prepared horseradish
1 teaspoon liquid smoke

Burgers
1 cup onion, coarsely chopped
1 can (15 ounces) no-salt-added kidney beans, rinsed and drained
½ heaping cup old-fashioned rolled oats
2 tablespoons flax meal

1 teaspoon garlic granules, or 2 cloves, smashed
¼ teaspoon freshly ground black pepper
¼ teaspoon powdered mustard
¼ teaspoon ground ginger
¼ teaspoon ground allspice
¼ teaspoon ground coriander
Pinch crushed red pepper flakes
Pinch ground cinnamon
Pinch ground cloves
1 tablespoon reduced-sodium tamari

Buns and Sauerkraut
4 burger buns, or 8 slices rye bread, toasted if desired
1 cup sauerkraut, well drained

TO MAKE THE DRESSING, put all the ingredients in a small bowl and whisk until well combined.

To make the burgers, put all the ingredients in a food processor in the order listed. Pulse 10 to 15 times, stopping to scrape down the work bowl two or three times with a silicone spatula, until well chopped but not puréed. Form into four equal patties.

To cook the burgers, mist a large, heavy skillet with cooking spray and heat over medium heat.

When hot, add the patties and cook until golden on the bottom, about 5 minutes. Flip and cook the other side until golden, about 5 minutes. (If the skillet doesn't hold all the burgers, cook them in batches.) Put each burger on a bun. Top with the sauerkraut and as much of the dressing as you like.

Per burger: 491 calories, 15 g protein, 23 g fat (2 g sat), 64 g carbohydrates, 1,142 mg sodium, 75 mg calcium, 11 g fiber

WHEN YOU TURN ON the oven to make something else (and the oven is set at 400 degrees F), be sure to roast a beet. That way, you can enjoy these sandwiches the next day with minimal preparation. The beet is earthy and a perfect complement to the tempeh. The crunchy romaine lettuce and creamy avocado take this sandwich over the top.

Beet, Lettuce, Tempeh, and Avocado Sandwiches

MAKES 4 SANDWICHES

1 beet (about the size of a baseball), scrubbed
1 avocado, sliced
8 slices bread, toasted if desired
¼ cup vegan mayonnaise
2 cups shredded romaine lettuce
1 recipe Better-than-Bacon Crumbles or Strips (page 77) or Better-than-Bacon Coconut Flakes (page 69)

PREHEAT THE OVEN to 400 degrees F. Wrap the beet in foil and put in a small ovenproof baking pan (in case the juices leak out). Bake for 1 hour. Let cool in the foil. Scrape off the beet skin over the sink, using the foil to help. Any tough bits can be cut away with a knife. Slice the beet as thinly as possible (preferably so thin you can see through it).

To assemble the sandwiches, arrange the avocado equally over four of the bread slices. Spread the mayonnaise on the remaining bread slices. Put the beet slices over the avocado, then add the lettuce, and then add the Better-than-Bacon Crumbles or Strips. Close with the remaining bread, spread-side in.

Per sandwich: 482 calories, 17 g protein, 29 g fat (5 g sat), 38 g carbohydrates, 663 mg sodium, 131 mg calcium, 6 g fiber

FUBONN IS AN ASIAN GROCERY store in Portland, Oregon, but we think of it as an enormous wonderland. You can purchase huge bunches of uncommon herbs and vegetables at great prices, find all sorts of amazing faux meats, discover new greens to fall in love with, and explore mysterious bottles of flavorings and sauces. These simple bowls combine a spectacular sauce with veggies that are available at your regular grocery store, but they deliver the delicious flavors of Fubonn.

Fubonn Bowls

MAKES 4 SERVINGS

6 cups cooked brown or white
    rice, hot
1 pound Unmarinated Go-To
    Tofu or Tempeh (page 68), hot
3 cups bite-sized broccoli florets,
    steamed until tender-crisp
3 cups cut green beans, in 2-inch
    pieces, steamed until
    tender-crisp
1 cup finely shredded red cabbage
1 cup grated carrot
1 cup Peanut-Hoisin Sauce
    (page 62)
Sriracha sauce or hot sauce

TO SERVE, DIVIDE THE RICE equally among four bowls. Put the tofu on one side of the bowl and the broccoli and green beans on the other side. Put the cabbage in the center and the carrot on top. Drizzle with the Peanut-Hoisin Sauce. Pass sriracha sauce at the table. Dig in!

Per serving: 661 calories, 22 g protein, 19 g fat (3 g sat), 101 g carbohydrates, 415 mg sodium, 129 mg calcium, 15 g fiber

Note: Analysis doesn't include sriracha or hot sauce to taste.

LOTS OF FOLKS THINK IT'S IMPOSSIBLE to make muffins without eggs or cookies without a pound of butter. We vegans know this isn't true. Now you can give cruelty-free baking a go with one of these ultra-simple and delicious treats. In this chapter you'll find recipes that run the gamut from savory and sweet to virtuous and healthy (and even a few that are downright decadent—this is a chapter on baked goods, after all!). Once you discover how delicious vegan baked goods can be, you'll wonder why anyone added animal products to them in the first place.

Baked Goods

Cranberry-Walnut Oat Bars, Page 162

THE TREATS WE EAT run more along the lines of quick breads and muffins than cookies and cupcakes. That means our treats are healthier, and I end up eating a lot less sugar. For Josh and Ruby, it means they can eat three times as many muffins as they would cookies! And while it's true we could all probably do with less sugar in our lives, you can still satisfy that sweet tooth without guilt. This bread should help you out in that department.

Mango Bread with Cardamom, Ginger, and Lime

MAKES 10 SLICES

1 cup plain or vanilla
   nondairy milk
2 tablespoons flax meal
1 lime, zest and juice (zest the
   lime before juicing)
2 cups white whole wheat flour
⅓ cup sugar
1½ teaspoons baking powder
1 teaspoon ground cardamom
½ teaspoon ground ginger
½ teaspoon baking soda
½ teaspoon salt
1½ cups finely chopped fresh or
   thawed frozen mango
3 tablespoons coconut oil,
   melted

PREHEAT THE OVEN to 350 degrees F. Oil a 9 x 5-inch loaf pan or mist with cooking spray.

Put the milk, flax meal, and lime juice in a medium bowl and stir to combine. Set aside to thicken, about 5 minutes.

Put the flour, sugar, baking powder, cardamom, ginger, baking soda, and salt in a large bowl. Whisk to combine.

Add the mango, oil, and lime zest to the milk mixture and stir well.

Pour the milk mixture into the flour mixture and stir until well combined. Pour into the prepared loaf pan and bake for 50 minutes, until a toothpick inserted in the center comes out clean. Let the bread cool in the pan. Remove from the pan to slice and serve.

Per slice: 142 calories, 3 g protein, 5 g fat (4 g sat), 23 g carbohydrates, 231 mg sodium, 62 mg calcium, 3 g fiber

SOMETIMES WE VEGANS try to make everything healthy. I admit it; I'm incredibly guilty of that. Sure, I can make a batch of muffins with super-healthy ingredients, and they'll taste just fine. But sometimes "fine" isn't enough. These muffins taste way better than "fine." They're vegan! They're muffins! And they're out of this world. Bake a batch, hand them out to your friends or coworkers or kids, and you'll make them feel extra special.

Perfect Berry Muffins

PREHEAT THE OVEN to 400 degrees F. Line a twelve-cup standard muffin tin with cupcake liners or mist with cooking spray.

Put the all-purpose flour, whole wheat flour, sugar, baking powder, baking soda, and salt in a large bowl and stir with a whisk to combine. Make a well in the middle and add the milk, oil, vinegar, and vanilla extract and stir to combine. Gently stir in the blueberries until evenly distributed.

Spoon into the lined muffin tin using ¼ cup of the batter for each muffin. Bake for 18 to 20 minutes, until a toothpick inserted in the center of a muffin comes out clean. Let cool in the muffin tin for 5 minutes. Then remove and let cool completely on a wire rack.

Tip: If using frozen berries, keep them in the freezer until just before you stir them into the batter. You will need to bake the muffins for a full 20 minutes when using frozen berries.

Per muffin: 174 calories, 4 g protein, 5 g fat (1 g sat), 28 g carbohydrates, 206 mg sodium, 67 mg calcium, 2 g fiber

MAKES 12 MUFFINS

1¼ cups unbleached all-purpose flour

1 cup white whole wheat flour

½ cup sugar

2 teaspoons baking powder

½ teaspoon baking soda

½ teaspoon salt

1¼ cup plain or vanilla nondairy milk

¼ cup vegetable oil

1 tablespoon cider vinegar

2 teaspoons vanilla extract

1½ cups fresh or frozen blueberries or raspberries or a mix (see tip)

THIS BREAD HAS IT ALL: chocolate, banana, whole grains, and vegetables. What? Vegetables? The bread is sweet enough to be a treat but not so sugary that you'll feel guilty going back for a second slice. For us, that's the sweet spot we aim for. You could easily replace the wheat flour with spelt or barley flour or a combination of the two, if that's your thing. The recipe would also work with all-purpose flour, but why miss out on the whole grains?

Chocolate–Chocolate Chip Zucchini–Banana Bread

MAKES 10 SLICES

2 cups white whole wheat flour

⅓ cup sugar

¼ cup unsweetened cocoa powder

2 teaspoons baking powder

½ teaspoon baking soda

½ teaspoon salt

1¼ cups plain or vanilla nondairy milk

½ cup mashed banana

2 tablespoons vegetable oil

1 teaspoon vanilla extract

1½ cups shredded zucchini or yellow squash

½ cup vegan semisweet chocolate chips

PREHEAT THE OVEN to 350 degrees F. Oil a 9 x 5-inch loaf pan or mist with cooking spray.

Put the flour, sugar, cocoa powder, baking powder, baking soda, and salt in a large bowl. Whisk to combine, breaking up any lumps of cocoa powder.

Put the milk, banana, oil, and vanilla extract in a medium bowl and whisk to combine. Stir in the zucchini. Pour the milk mixture into the flour mixture and stir to combine. Stir in the chocolate chips.

Pour into the prepared loaf pan. Bake for 45 to 50 minutes, until a toothpick inserted in the center comes out clean. Let the bread cool in the pan. Remove from the pan to slice and serve.

Per slice: 208 calories, 5 g protein, 7 g fat (2 g sat), 33 g carbohydrates, 245 mg sodium, 79 mg calcium, 4 g fiber

FOR SO MUCH OF THE YEAR, apples and pears are the best fruits around, and this recipe really makes the most of them. These muffins are perfectly sweet and full of healthy ingredients yet still light. That's what I love most about them.

Multigrain Apple Muffins

PREHEAT THE OVEN to 400 degrees F. Line a twelve-cup standard muffin tin with cupcake liners or mist with cooking spray.

Put the flour, sugar, flax meal, baking powder, cinnamon, baking soda, and salt in a large bowl and stir with a whisk to combine. Make a well in the middle and add the milk, oil, and vanilla extract and stir to combine. Stir in the apples. The mixture will seem very dry, but keep stirring to distribute the moisture evenly through the batter. Spoon into the lined muffin tin using ¼ cup of the batter for each muffin. Bake for 16 to 18 minutes, until a toothpick inserted in the center of a muffin comes out clean. Let cool in the muffin tin for 5 minutes. Then remove and let cool completely on a wire rack.

Multigrain Pear Muffins: Replace the apples with an equal amount of chopped pears.

Per muffin: 160 calories, 3 g protein, 5 g fat (0.3 g sat), 25 g carbohydrates, 172 mg sodium, 47 mg calcium, 4 g fiber

MAKES 12 MUFFINS

1¾ cups spelt flour or white whole wheat flour
½ cup sugar
⅓ cup flax meal
2 teaspoons baking powder
1 teaspoon ground cinnamon
½ teaspoon baking soda
½ teaspoon salt
½ cup plain or vanilla nondairy milk
3 tablespoons vegetable oil
1 tablespoon vanilla extract
1½ cups very finely chopped apples (about 2 small; peeling optional)

THESE MUFFINS ARE a great sidekick to any kind of chili or soup. They have a wee bit of spice, courtesy of the pickled jalapeños, which also add a pleasant hint of salt and vinegar. It's fun to eat three of these muffins at a time, as soon as they're cool enough. Or maybe that's just us?

Spicy Corn Muffins

MAKES 12 MUFFINS

1¼ cups plain nondairy milk
¼ cup vegetable oil
¼ cup maple syrup
¼ cup chopped pickled
    jalapeño chiles
3 tablespoons chopped
    fresh cilantro
2 tablespoons lime juice
1¼ cups yellow cornmeal
1 cup unbleached all-purpose
    flour
2 teaspoons baking powder
1 teaspoon baking soda
½ teaspoon salt

PREHEAT THE OVEN to 400 degrees F. Line a twelve-cup standard muffin tin with cupcake liners or mist with cooking spray.

Put the milk, oil, maple syrup, chiles, cilantro, and lime juice in a small bowl and stir to combine. Put the cornmeal, flour, baking powder, baking soda, and salt in a large bowl and whisk to combine. Make a well in the middle and pour in the milk mixture. Stir until just combined (don't overmix).

Spoon into the lined muffin tin using ¼ cup of the batter for each muffin. Bake for 18 to 20 minutes, until a toothpick inserted in the center of a muffin comes out clean. Let cool in the muffin tin for 5 minutes. Then remove and let cool completely on a wire rack.

Per muffin: 150 calories, 3 g protein, 6 g fat (1 g sat), 23 g carbohydrates, 212 mg sodium, 67 mg calcium, 2 g fiber

SIX OUT OF TEN Herbivore fans call cornbread their favorite side dish. We agree. A reliable cornbread recipe is a must-have for every vegan cook. If you have a ten-inch cast iron skillet, you absolutely must use it for this recipe.

Classic Skillet Cornbread

MAKES 8 SERVINGS

1½ cups yellow cornmeal
1½ cups white whole wheat flour or unbleached all-purpose flour
1 tablespoon baking powder
1 teaspoon salt
2 cups plain nondairy milk
¼ cup vegetable oil
¼ cup agave nectar or maple syrup

PREHEAT THE OVEN to 400 degrees F. Oil a 10-inch cast iron skillet or an 8-inch square glass baking dish.

Put the cornmeal, flour, baking powder, and salt in a large bowl and whisk to combine. Make a well in the middle and add the milk, oil, and agave nectar. Stir until just combined (don't overmix). Pour into the prepared skillet or baking dish. If using a cast iron skillet, bake for 30 minutes. If using a glass baking dish, bake for 25 minutes. Let cool for 5 minutes before slicing.

Per serving: 272 calories, 7 g protein, 9 g fat (1 g sat), 41 g carbohydrates, 418 mg sodium, 151 mg calcium, 5 g fiber

I AM WAY TOO LAZY to make a pie! A crisp is where it's at, if you ask me. Any time of year, there is a fresh or frozen fruit begging to be put in a crisp. Crisps can be easily customized and easily veganized, and everybody loves a crisp topped with ice cream. Be virtuous and make this crisp as written, or be as naughty as you want and add more coconut oil, vegan butter, and sugar.

Ginger Peach Crisp

PREHEAT THE OVEN to 375 degrees F. Oil an 8-inch square baking pan and set aside.

Chop the peaches into bite-sized pieces and put them in a medium bowl. Add the agave nectar, cornstarch, and ginger and toss to coat. Spoon into the prepared baking pan.

In the same bowl, put the oats, almonds, flour, brown sugar, oil, Cashew Cream, cinnamon, and salt. Stir well until the mixture becomes crumbly. Sprinkle evenly over the peaches. Bake for 35 to 40 minutes, until the topping is browned and the peaches are bubbling.

Per serving: 320 calories, 5 g protein, 17 g fat (9 g sat), 38 g carbohydrates, 104 mg sodium, 8 mg calcium, 4 g fiber

MAKES 6 SERVINGS

1 bag (1 pound) frozen sliced peaches, partially thawed
2 tablespoons agave nectar
1 tablespoon cornstarch
2 teaspoons grated fresh ginger
1 cup old-fashioned rolled oats
½ cup finely ground almonds
¼ cup unbleached all-purpose flour, whole wheat flour, or white whole wheat flour
¼ cup light brown sugar, lightly packed
¼ cup coconut oil, melted
2 tablespoons Cashew Cream (page 56) or plain or vanilla nondairy milk
½ teaspoon ground cinnamon
¼ teaspoon salt

THESE BARS ARE PERFECT to take on an epic bike ride or to keep the kids energized during a fun day at the beach or pool. They're also terrific in a lunch box (if you aren't the outdoorsy type). Honestly, raw nuts and dried fruits shouldn't be this delicious. But once you combine them with vanilla and incredibly sweet dates, you'll never buy an energy bar again.

Cranberry-Walnut Oat Bars

MAKES 8 BARS

1 cup walnuts
1 cup old-fashioned rolled oats
½ cup dried cranberries
½ cup pitted soft dates
1 teaspoon vanilla extract
Pinch salt
1 teaspoon water, plus
    more as needed

PUT THE WALNUTS, oats, cranberries, dates, vanilla extract, and salt in a food processor and pulse until finely ground and starting to stick together. If the mixture doesn't stick together, add the water and pulse again. The mixture should hold together when pressed between your fingers. If necessary, add more water and pulse again.

Put a sheet of waxed paper on a flat surface and turn the mixture out onto it. Form the mixture into an 8-inch square with your hands (moisten them with water if necessary to prevent sticking) and cut into 8 bars. Wrap each bar tightly with plastic wrap and store in the refrigerator.

Per bar: 205 calories, 4 g protein, 11 g fat (0.1 g sat), 25 g carbohydrates, 0 mg sodium, 20 mg calcium, 3 g fiber

CONSIDER THESE BARS a fancy version of the Cranberry-Walnut Oat Bars on page 162. While they're just as easy to prepare, they're also a little show-offy, what with their hazelnuts, hemp seeds, and cherries.

Hazelnut, Hemp, and Cherry Oat Bars

PUT THE OATS, dates, hazelnuts, pecans, hemp seeds, cherries, vanilla extract, and salt in a food processor and pulse until finely ground and starting to stick together. If the mixture doesn't stick together, add the water and pulse again. The mixture should hold together when pressed between your fingers. If necessary, add more water and pulse again.

Put a sheet of waxed paper on a flat surface and turn the mixture out onto it. Form the mixture into an 8-inch square with your hands (moisten them with water if necessary to prevent sticking) and cut into 8 bars. Wrap each bar tightly with plastic wrap and store in the refrigerator.

Per bar: 161 calories, 4 g protein, 7 g fat (1 g sat), 21 g carbohydrates, 1 mg sodium, 19 mg calcium, 3 g fiber

MAKES 8 BARS

1 cup old-fashioned rolled oats
½ cup pitted soft dates
¼ cup hazelnuts
¼ cup pecans
¼ cup hemp seeds
¼ cup dried cherries
1½ teaspoons vanilla extract
Pinch salt
1 teaspoon water, plus more
   as needed

THIS RECIPE IS A cross between healthy granola bars and no-bake treats. Sweet but not too sweet, these bars are special enough to satisfy my sweets-obsessed child. For an extra-special version, replace the raisins with chocolate chips. Once you get the basic version down, feel free to get creative.

Real Chewy Granola Bars

LINE A 13 X 9-INCH baking pan with foil, allowing a 1-inch overhang. Mist the foil with cooking spray.

Put the peanut butter, milk, and rice syrup in a large saucepan. Bring to a boil over medium-high heat, stirring constantly, until well combined, 2 to 3 minutes. Stir in the vanilla extract and salt and remove from the heat. Add the oats, cereal, raisins, almonds, and flax meal and stir with a silicone spatula until well combined.

Scoop into the lined pan, pressing down with the spatula or with lightly moistened hands. Spread it evenly and press firmly. Use some muscle!

Cover and refrigerate for at least 1 hour (but preferably longer). This will keep the bars from falling apart.

Lift the bars out of the pan with the foil and transfer to a cutting board. Cut the bars into squares or rectangles using a sharp knife. Store in a tightly sealed container in the refrigerator.

Variation: Add ¼ teaspoon of ground cinnamon or cardamom.

Per bar: 225 calories, 6 g protein, 12 g fat (6 g sat), 27 g carbohydrates, 92 mg sodium, 16 mg calcium, 4 g fiber

MAKES 8 BARS

¾ cup unsalted natural peanut butter or other nut butter
½ cup plain or vanilla nondairy milk
¼ cup brown rice syrup
1½ teaspoons vanilla extract
¼ teaspoon salt
2 cups old-fashioned rolled oats or barley flakes
2 cups crispy rice cereal
½ cup raisins
¼ cup finely ground almonds
¼ cup flax meal

YOU HAVE AMY WHO works with us at Herbivore to thank for this recipe. If you have purchased anything from our website, it's likely that Amy packed your order. She loves to cook and bake and admittedly has a thing for brownies. A seriously big thing for brownies. When you come across people who think that vegans are deprived, just pop one of these morsels in their mouths. That'll silence 'em.

Fudgy Brownies

MAKES 9 LARGE OR 16 SMALL BROWNIES

⅔ cup warm water
3 tablespoons flax meal
½ cup vegan butter
½ cup vegan semisweet chocolate chips
1¼ cups sugar
2¼ teaspoons vanilla extract
1⅓ cups whole wheat pastry flour
½ cup unsweetened Dutch-processed cocoa powder, sifted
¾ teaspoon baking powder
Scant ½ teaspoon salt

PREHEAT THE OVEN to 350 degrees F. Lightly oil an 8-inch square baking pan.

Put the water and flax meal in a small bowl and whisk to combine. Set aside to thicken, about 5 minutes.

Put the butter and chocolate chips in a small saucepan. Heat over low heat, stirring constantly, until melted and smooth. Transfer to a large bowl. Add the flax mixture, sugar, and vanilla extract and stir to combine.

Put the flour, cocoa powder, baking powder, and salt in a medium bowl and stir to combine. Add the flour mixture to the chocolate mixture and stir until no flour is visible and the batter is smooth and very thick. Spread into the prepared baking pan using a silicone spatula.

Bake for 24 minutes if using a metal pan, or for 28 minutes if using a glass pan, or until a toothpick inserted halfway between the center and the edge of the pan comes out with just a few crumbs attached (there shouldn't be any wet batter clinging to the toothpick). The center won't look set, but don't worry; that's how it's supposed to look.

Cool in the pan on a wire rack. Once cool, put the pan in the refrigerator so the brownies set properly. Don't skip this step! It's what creates the fudgy goodness. Cut into squares and serve. Cover and store any leftover brownies in the refrigerator.

Per large brownie: 329 calories, 4 g protein, 14 g fat (5 g sat), 51 g carbohydrates, 180 mg sodium, 33 mg calcium, 5 g fiber

THIS AMAZING COOKIE is a version of a Julie Hasson recipe. Julie has written many cookbooks and founded Native Bowl, a popular food cart in Portland. Her baking prowess is legendary. When I first made these cookies, I shared one with my neighbor, who promptly exclaimed, "This cookie is worth the price of the book!" I knew we had a winner. These are serious cookies for serious cookie lovers.

Cappuccino-Orange Chocolate Chip Cookies

PREHEAT THE OVEN to 350 degrees F. Line two baking sheets with parchment paper.

Put the water and flax meal in a small bowl or measuring cup and stir to combine. Set aside to thicken, about 5 minutes.

Put the flour, coffee beans, baking powder, baking soda, cinnamon, and salt in a medium bowl and stir to combine.

Put the brown sugar, oil, vanilla extract, orange zest, and reserved flax mixture in a large bowl and stir until smooth and well combined. Add the flour mixture, stirring until just combined. Stir in the oats, chocolate chips, and milk just until evenly distributed.

Use ¼ cup of dough for each cookie. Arrange the dough on the lined baking sheets at least four inches apart to allow the cookies to spread. Press the cookies down with the heel of your hand until they are about ½ inch thick. Bake for 14 minutes, until puffed and golden brown (they'll still be soft to the touch). Let cool completely on the baking sheet before removing.

Per cookie: 305 calories, 4 g protein, 12 g fat (4 g sat), 49 g carbohydrates, 177 mg sodium, 50 mg calcium, 2 g fiber

MAKES 12 LARGE COOKIES

3 tablespoons hot water
1 tablespoon flax meal
1¾ cups unbleached all-purpose flour
1 tablespoon finely ground coffee beans
1½ teaspoons baking powder
¾ teaspoon baking soda
½ teaspoon ground cinnamon
¼ teaspoon salt
1¼ cups brown sugar, packed
⅓ cup vegetable oil
1½ teaspoons vanilla extract
1 teaspoon orange zest
1 cup old-fashioned rolled oats
1 cup vegan semisweet chocolate chips
¼ cup plain or vanilla nondairy milk

Cappuccino-Orange Chocolate Chip Cookies, Page 167

Sweetpea Snickerdoodles, Page 169

SWEETPEA BAKING COMPANY is our neighbor at the vegan mini-mall. People from all over the world make the pilgrimage to our little row of shops, and countless visitors have asked me, "How can you work next to that place without eating sweets all day?" When we first opened, that was definitely a problem. I've since learned to control myself . . . a little. Asking Sweetpea for this recipe was a no-brainer. Friends, I present the best snickerdoodle you have ever eaten!

Sweetpea Snickerdoodles

PREHEAT THE OVEN to 350 degrees F. Line two baking sheets with parchment paper.

Put the flour, cream of tartar, baking soda, and salt in a medium bowl and stir to combine.

Put the sugar and vegan butter in a large bowl and cream together until smooth. Add the water and egg-replacer powder and stir with a silicone spatula. Add the flour mixture and stir until well combined. The mixture will seem dry at first, but keep stirring.

Use ¼ cup of dough for each large cookie or 2 tablespoons of dough for each small cookie. Arrange the dough on the lined baking sheets at least four inches apart to allow the cookies to spread. Flatten slightly with the heel of your hand. Sprinkle with the cinnamon sugar. Bake for 14 minutes, until golden. Let cool on the baking sheet for 5 minutes, then transfer to a wire rack to cool completely.

Tips: Ener-G Egg Replacer powder is a commercial egg replacer. It is available at many grocery stores and sometimes can be found in the bulk section of well-stocked natural food markets. It's convenient to have on hand to veganize conventional baking recipes.

If you don't have access to prepared cinnamon sugar or simply prefer to make your own, put 1 tablespoon of sugar and 1 teaspoon of ground cinnamon in a small bowl or cup and stir until well combined.

Per large cookie: 282 calories, 3 g protein, 11 g fat (3 g sat), 42 g carbohydrates, 293 mg sodium, 20 mg calcium, 1 g fiber

MAKES 8 LARGE OR 16 SMALL COOKIES

1¾ cups unbleached all-purpose flour

1 teaspoon cream of tartar

¾ teaspoon baking soda

¼ teaspoon salt

¾ cup sugar

½ cup vegan butter, softened

¼ cup water

1½ teaspoons Ener-G Egg Replacer powder (see tip)

1 tablespoon plus 1 teaspoon cinnamon sugar (see tip)

SOMETIMES A PERSON (and by "person" I mean me) just wants delicious, cheesy white bread, and there's nothing wrong with that. This recipe is part pizza, part pull-apart bread, and all addictively yummy. If you opt to make sixteen little stacks, they'll be perfect for after-school (or after-work) treats. Serve the big stacks at dinner to accompany a bowl of soup or a gigantic salad. The stacks require a little bit of work in the kitchen, but they're totally worth it.

Savory Pull-Apart Bread Stacks

TO MAKE THE DOUGH, put the water, yeast, and sugar in a small cup. Stir to combine. Set aside until foamy, about 5 minutes.

Put the flour and salt in a large bowl and whisk to combine.

Add the oil to the yeast mixture and stir to combine. Pour into the flour mixture and stir until all the flour is incorporated. Knead in the bowl for 1 to 2 minutes. Form into a large ball.

Mist a large bowl with cooking spray. Put the dough in the bowl, cover with a clean kitchen towel, and set aside until doubled, 1 to 2 hours. Punch down the dough and knead it in the bowl for 30 seconds. Divide the dough in half and let it rest for 15 minutes.

Preheat the oven to 425 degrees F. Line a baking sheet with parchment paper.

To make the topping, put the oil, garlic, vinegar, and salt in a small bowl and stir to combine.

To make the stacks, generously flour a flat work surface or counter. Using a rolling pin, roll out half the dough into a 12-inch square. Make sure you can pick up the dough and it isn't sticking to the work surface. Spread half the oil mixture evenly over the dough. Sprinkle with half the spinach, half the tomato, and half the cheese, in that order. For large stacks, cut into 4-inch squares by making three cuts vertically and three cuts horizontally (like a tic-tac-toe board), using a dough scraper or butter knife. For small stacks, cut into 2-inch squares.

Carefully stack three pieces of dough on top of each other. The dough can be at angles; it doesn't have to be stacked perfectly. Transfer each stack to the lined baking sheet. Repeat with the remaining dough and topping ingredients. Bake for 16 to 18 minutes, until the cheese is melted and the edges are brown.

Per 4-inch stack: 324 calories, 7 g protein, 14 g fat (3 g sat), 44 g carbohydrates, 478 mg sodium, 12 mg calcium, 3 g fiber

MAKES EIGHT 4-INCH STACKS OR SIXTEEN 2-INCH STACKS

Dough
1¼ cups warm water
2¼ teaspoons (1 packet) active dry yeast
1 teaspoon sugar
3 cups unbleached all-purpose flour
1 teaspoon salt
1 tablespoon olive oil

Topping
¼ cup olive oil
1 tablespoon minced garlic
2 teaspoons balsamic vinegar
Pinch salt
½ cup finely chopped spinach
½ cup finely chopped tomato
1½ cups shredded vegan cheese

THIS RECIPE FALLS into the category of celebration food. Bread cooked with chocolate and bananas and then doused with cinnamon and sugar? This is what you make when it's time to party. Did you just win the lottery? Whip this up. Graduate from somewhere? This is your thing. Finish in the top fifty thousand in the Chicago Marathon? You've earned this. If you don't need an excuse to celebrate, make this more often.

Chocolate Chip–Banana Bread Pudding

MAKES 6 SERVINGS

1 banana, well mashed
1½ cups plain or vanilla
   nondairy milk
½ cup raisins
¼ cup sugar
¼ cup finely ground almonds
2 teaspoons vanilla extract
1 teaspoon ground cinnamon
5 cups cubed day-old bread
1 banana, sliced
½ cup vegan semisweet chocolate chips

PREHEAT THE OVEN to 350 degrees F. Mist an 8-inch square baking pan with cooking spray.

Put the mashed banana in a large bowl. Add the milk, raisins, sugar, almonds, vanilla extract, and cinnamon and whisk until well combined. Add the bread cubes and stir until evenly coated. Add the sliced banana and chocolate chips and stir until evenly distributed. Pour into the prepared baking pan and cover with foil. Bake for 40 minutes. Uncover and bake for 10 minutes longer. Let cool for 5 minutes before digging in.

Per serving: 308 calories, 4 g protein, 8 g fat (3 g sat), 39 g carbohydrates, 32 mg sodium, 86 mg calcium, 3 g fiber

Resources

HERE IS A SHORT LIST of highly recommended books and websites that we use and find indispensable.

BOOKS

Becoming Vegan, Express Edition by Brenda Davis and Vesanto Melina

Going Vegan by Joni Marie Newman and Gerrie L. Adams

Green is the New Red by Will Potter

How to Be Vegan by Elizabeth Castoria

Vegan for Her by Virginia Messina

Vegan for Life by Jack Norris and Virginia Messina

Vegan Pregnancy Survival Guide by Sayward Rebhal

ORGANIZATIONS AND WEBSITES

farmsanctuary.org

Farm Sanctuary is committed to ending cruelty to farm animals and promoting compassionate vegan living through rescue, education, and advocacy efforts.

foodispower.org

The Food Empowerment Project is where human rights and animal rights meet.

mercyforanimals.org

Mercy for Animals is dedicated to preventing cruelty to farmed animals and promoting compassionate food choices and policies.

nutritionfacts.org

This site offers short, easy-to-understand videos by Michael Greger, MD, that explain the science behind nutrition studies.

ourhenhouse.org

This multimedia organization produces resources that you can use to find your own way to create change for animals.

pcrm.org

The Physicians Committee for Responsible Medicine promotes healthful vegan diets for disease prevention and works to end the use of animals in education and experiments.

theveganrd.com

Virginia Messina's straightforward blog discusses ethical veganism from a registered dietitian's perspective.

vegan.com

This all-inclusive site is a great resource for all things vegan, from living as a vegan to shopping.

veganhealth.org

This offshoot of Vegan Outreach (see below) provides nutrition recommendations and tips.

veganoutreach.org

Vegan Outreach works to end cruelty to animals.

vegbooks.org

Vegbooks provides a comprehensive resource for parents by parents, with reviews of children's books, movies, and other media from a veg perspective, along with many other helpful veg parenting links.

Acknowledgments

THANK YOU TO Ruby Hooten, Tracy Harrison, Remy Holladay, Amy Gedgaudas, Ginny Messina, Annie Shannon, Gene Baur, Miyoko Schinner, Anonymous, Julie Hasson, Joanna Vaught, Wendy Gabbe-Day, Lisa Higgins, and every Herbivore customer ever!

We are grateful to Jeanette Zeis (jeanettezeis.com) for the pottery used in many photos.

A gigantic thank you to Bob and everyone at Book Publishing Company.

Special thanks and huge gratitude to all of our activist friends for fighting the good fight and keeping us motivated to always try to do more.

Index

About the Authors

MICHELLE SCHWEGMAN AND JOSH HOOTEN live in the veganopolis of Portland, Oregon. From publishing books and magazines to organizing and attending animal rights and vegetarian conferences and festivals nationwide, this dynamic duo has converted their passion for a compassionate lifestyle into their livelihood. Their store is part of the world's only vegan mini-mall, along with Sweetpea Baking Company, Food Fight Vegan Grocery, and Scapegoat Tattoo. They carry their own clothing line as well as hundreds of vegan cookbooks, jewelry, body-care items, kitchen gadgets, scarves, socks, non-leather bags, wallets, and belts (including those from their own US-made line, Be Kind), and much more.

photos: Amy Gedgaudas

Keep up!
herbivoreclothing.com
instagram.com/herbivoreclothing
facebook.com/herbivoreclothingcompany

BookPublishing CO.

books that educate, inspire, and empower

To find your favorite books on plant-based cooking and nutrition,
living foods lifestyle, and healthy living, visit:

BookPubCo.com

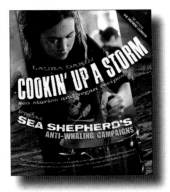

Cookin' Up A Storm
Laura Dakin
978-1-57067-312-2 • $24.95

Leff Love
Kittee Berns
978-1-57067-311-5 • $19.95

The Ayurvedic Vegan Kitchen
Talya Lutzker
978-1-57067-286-6 • $19.95

Artisan Vegan Cheese
Miyoko Schinner
978-1-57067-283-5 • $19.95

Becoming Vegan: Express Edition
Brenda Davis, RD,
Vesanto Melina, MS, RD
978-1-57067-295-8 • $19.95

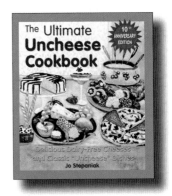

The Ultimate Uncheese Cookbook
Jo Stepaniak
978-1-57067-151-7 • $19.95

Purchase these health titles and cookbooks from your local bookstore or natural food store,
or you can buy them directly from:

Book Publishing Company • P.O. Box 99 • Summertown, TN 38483 • 1-888-260-8458

Please include $3.95 per book for shipping and handling.